GOOD
TOLD B

Today's English Version

THE BIBLE SOCIETIES

COLLINS/FOUNT

Printed in Great Britain
Collins Clear-Type Press
London and Glasgow

English-TEV Matthew
© American Bible Society
New York 1966, 1971 and 4th edition 1976
BFBS/NBSS - 1978 - 50M - TEV560P
ISBN 0 564 06761 X

Outline of Contents

Several hundred years ago, the Bible was divided into chapters and verses to make it easy to refer to. The Good News Bible, from which 'Good News Told by Matthew' is taken, has kept to this system. For example, 1.1—2.23 equals chapter 1, verse 1 to chapter 2, verse 23.

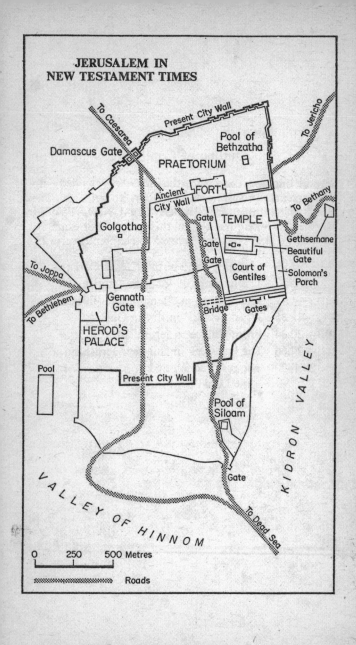

JERUSALEM IN
NEW TESTAMENT TIMES

To Caesarea

Present City Wall

To Jericho

Damascus Gate

Pool of
Bethzatha

PRAETORIUM

FORT

Ancient
City Wall

TEMPLE

To Bethany

Gate

Golgotha

Gate

Gethsemane

Gate

Beautiful
Gate

Court of
Gentiles

Solomon's
Porch

Gennath
Gate

Bridge

Gates

HEROD'S
PALACE

Present City Wall

Pool

Pool of
Siloam

Gate

To Joppa

To Bethlehem

KIDRON VALLEY

VALLEY OF HINNOM

To Dead Sea

0   250   500 Metres

Roads

INTRODUCTION

The Gospel of Matthew tells the good news that Jesus is the promised Saviour, the one through whom God fulfilled the promises he made to his people in the Old Testament. This good news is not only for the Jewish people, among whom Jesus was born and lived, but for the whole world.

Matthew is carefully arranged. It begins with the birth of Jesus, describes his baptism and temptation, and then takes up his ministry of preaching, teaching, and healing in Galilee. After this the Gospel records Jesus' journey from Galilee to Jerusalem and the events of Jesus' last week, culminating in his crucifixion and resurrection.

This Gospel presents Jesus as the great Teacher, who has the authority to interpret the Law of God, and who teaches about God's kingdom. Much of his teaching is gathered by subject matter into five collections: (1) the Sermon on the Mount, which concerns the character, duties, privileges, and destiny of the citizens of the Kingdom of heaven (chapters 5–7); (2) instructions to the twelve disciples for their mission (chapter 10); (3) parables about the Kingdom of heaven (chapter 13); (4) teaching on the meaning of discipleship (chapter 18); and (5) teaching about the end of the present age and the coming of the Kingdom of heaven (chapters 24–25).

GOOD NEWS
TOLD BY MATTHEW

The Ancestors of Jesus Christ
(Luke 3.23-38)

1 This is the list of the ancestors of Jesus Christ, a descendant of David, who was a descendant of Abraham.

2-6a From Abraham to King David, the following ancestors are listed: Abraham, Isaac, Jacob, Judah and his brothers; then Perez and Zerah (their mother was Tamar), Hezron, Ram, Amminadab, Nahshon, Salmon, Boaz (his mother was Rahab), Obed (his mother was Ruth), Jesse, and King David.

6b-11 From David to the time when the people of Israel were taken into exile in Babylon, the following ancestors are listed: David, Solomon (his mother was the woman who had been Uriah's wife), Rehoboam, Abijah, Asa, Jehoshaphat, Jehoram, Uzziah, Jotham, Ahaz, Hezekiah, Manasseh, Amon, Josiah, and Jehoiachin and his brothers.

12-16 From the time after the exile in Babylon to the birth of Jesus, the following ancestors are listed: Jehoiachin, Shealtiel, Zerubbabel, Abiud, Eliakim, Azor, Zadok, Achim, Eliud, Eleazar, Matthan, Jacob, and Joseph, who married Mary, the mother of Jesus, who was called the Messiah.

17 So then, there were fourteen generations from Abraham to David, and fourteen from David to the exile in Babylon, and fourteen from then to the birth of the Messiah.

The Birth of Jesus Christ
(Luke 2.1-7)

18 This was how the birth of Jesus Christ took place. His mother Mary was engaged to Joseph, but before they were married, she found out that she was going to have a baby by the Holy Spirit. 19 Joseph

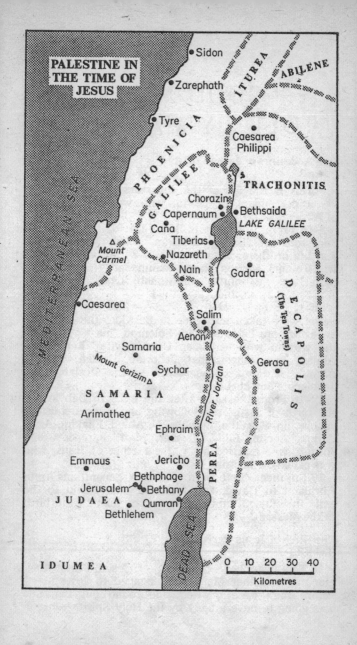

PALESTINE IN THE TIME OF JESUS

MEDITERRANEAN SEA

• Sidon

• Zarephath

ITUREA

ABILENE

PHOENICIA

• Tyre

• Caesarea Philippi

GALILEE

TRACHONITIS

• Chorazin

• Capernaum

• Bethsaida

LAKE GALILEE

• Cana

• Tiberias

△ Mount Carmel

• Nazareth

• Nain

• Gadara

D E C A P O L I S (The Ten Towns)

• Caesarea

• Salim

• Aenon

• Samaria

• Gerasa

Mount Gerizim △ • Sychar

River Jordan

S A M A R I A

• Arimathea

• Ephraim

PEREA

• Emmaus

• Jericho

• Bethphage

Jerusalem • • Bethany

J U D A E A • Qumran

• Bethlehem

DEAD SEA

I D U M E A

0 10 20 30 40

Kilometres

was a man who always did what was right, but he did not want to disgrace Mary publicly; so he made plans to break the engagement privately. ²⁰While he was thinking about this, an angel of the Lord appeared to him in a dream and said, "Joseph, descendant of David, do not be afraid to take Mary to be your wife. For it is by the Holy Spirit that she has conceived. ²¹She will have a son, and you will name him Jesus— because he will save his people from their sins."

22 Now all this happened in order to make what the Lord had said through the prophet come true, ²³"A virgin will become pregnant and have a son, and he will be called Immanuel" (which means, "God is with us").

24 So when Joseph woke up, he married Mary, as the angel of the Lord had told him to do. ²⁵But he had no sexual relations with her before she gave birth to her son. And Joseph named him Jesus.

Visitors from the East

2 Jesus was born in the town of Bethlehem in Judaea, during the time when Herod was king. Soon afterwards, some men who studied the stars came from the east to Jerusalem ²and asked, "Where is the baby born to be the king of the Jews? We saw his star when it came up in the east, and we have come to worship him."

3 When King Herod heard about this, he was very upset, and so was everyone else in Jerusalem. ⁴He called together all the chief priests and the teachers of the Law and asked them, "Where will the Messiah be born?"

5 "In the town of Bethlehem in Judaea," they answered. "For this is what the prophet wrote:
⁶'Bethlehem in the land of Judah,
     you are by no means the least of the leading
          cities of Judah;
     for from you will come a leader
     who will guide my people Israel.' "
7 So Herod called the visitors from the east to a secret meeting and found out from them the exact time the star had appeared. ⁸Then he sent them to Bethlehem with these instructions: "Go and make a

careful search for the child, and when you find him, let me know, so that I too may go and worship him."

The same star...went ahead of them (2.9-10)

9-10 And so they left, and on their way they saw the same star they had seen in the east. When they saw it, how happy they were, what joy was theirs! It went ahead of them until it stopped over the place where the child was. 11 They went into the house, and when they saw the child with his mother Mary, they knelt down and worshipped him. They brought out their gifts of gold, frankincense, and myrrh, and presented them to him.

12 Then they returned to their country by another road, since God had warned them in a dream not to go back to Herod.

The Escape to Egypt

13 After they had left, an angel of the Lord appeared in a dream to Joseph and said, "Herod will be looking for the child in order to kill him. So get up, take the child and his mother and escape to Egypt, and stay there until I tell you to leave."

14 Joseph got up, took the child and his mother,

and left during the night for Egypt, [15]where he stayed until Herod died. This was done to make what the Lord had said through the prophet come true, "I called my Son out of Egypt."

The Killing of the Children

16 When Herod realized that the visitors from the east had tricked him, he was furious. He gave orders to kill all the boys in Bethlehem and its neighbourhood who were two years old and younger—this was done in accordance with what he had learned from the visitors about the time when the star had appeared.

17 In this way what the prophet Jeremiah had said came true:

[18] "A sound is heard in Ramah,
    the sound of bitter weeping.
Rachel is crying for her children;
    she refuses to be comforted,
    for they are dead."

The Return from Egypt

19 After Herod died, an angel of the Lord appeared in a dream to Joseph in Egypt [20]and said, "Get up, take the child and his mother, and go back to the land of Israel, because those who tried to kill the child are dead." [21]So Joseph got up, took the child and his mother, and went back to Israel.

22 But when Joseph heard that Archelaus had succeeded his father Herod as king of Judaea, he was afraid to go there. He was given more instructions in a dream, so he went to the province of Galilee [23]and made his home in a town named Nazareth. And so what the prophets had said came true: "He will be called a Nazarene."

The Preaching of John the Baptist
(Mark 1.1-8; Luke 3.1-18; John 1.19-28)

3 At that time John the Baptist came to the desert of Judaea and started preaching. [2]"Turn away from your sins," he said, "because the Kingdom of heaven is near!" [3]John was the man the prophet Isaiah was talking about when he said,

"Someone is shouting in the desert,

'Prepare a road for the Lord;
make a straight path for him to travel!' "

4 John's clothes were made of camel's hair; he wore a leather belt round his waist, and his food was locusts and wild honey. 5People came to him from Jerusalem, from the whole province of Judaea, and from all the country near the River Jordan. 6They confessed their sins, and he baptized them in the Jordan.

7 When John saw many Pharisees and Sadducees coming to him to be baptized, he said to them, "You snakes—who told you that you could escape from the punishment God is about to send? 8Do those things that will show that you have turned from your sins. 9And don't think you can escape punishment by saying that Abraham is your ancestor. I tell you that God can take these stones and make descendants for Abraham! 10The axe is ready to cut down the trees at the roots; every tree that does not bear good fruit will be cut down and thrown in the fire. 11I baptize you with water to show that you have repented, but the one who will come after me will baptize you with the Holy Spirit and fire. He is much greater than I am; and I am not good enough even to carry his sandals. 12He has his winnowing shovel with him to thresh out all the grain. He will gather his wheat into his barn, but he will burn the chaff in a fire that never goes out."

The Baptism of Jesus
(Mark 1.9–11; Luke 3.21–22)

13 At that time Jesus arrived from Galilee and came to John at the Jordan to be baptized by him. 14But John tried to make him change his mind. "I ought to be baptized by you," John said, "and yet you have come to me!"

15 But Jesus answered him, "Let it be so for now. For in this way we shall do all that God requires." So John agreed.

16 As soon as Jesus was baptized, he came up out of the water. Then heaven was opened to him, and he saw the Spirit of God coming down like a dove and alighting on him. 17Then a voice said from

heaven, "This is my own dear Son, with whom I am pleased."

The Temptation of Jesus
(Mark 1.12–13; Luke 4.1–13)

4 Then the Spirit led Jesus into the desert to be tempted by the Devil. ²After spending forty days and nights without food, Jesus was hungry. ³Then

Order these stones to turn into bread (4.3)

the Devil came to him and said, "If you are God's Son, order these stones to turn into bread."

4 But Jesus answered, "The scripture says, 'Man cannot live on bread alone, but needs every word that God speaks.' "

5 Then the Devil took Jesus to Jerusalem, the Holy City, set him on the highest point of the Temple, ⁶and said to him, "If you are God's Son, throw yourself down, for the scripture says,

'God will give orders to his angels about you;
　they will hold you up with their hands,

so that not even your feet will be hurt on the
stones.' "

7 Jesus answered, "But the scripture also says, 'Do
not put the Lord your God to the test.' "

8 Then the Devil took Jesus to a very high mountain
and showed him all the kingdoms of the world in
all their greatness. 9 "All this I will give you," the
Devil said, "if you kneel down and worship me."

10 Then Jesus answered, "Go away, Satan! The scripture says, 'Worship the Lord your God and serve
only him!' "

11 Then the Devil left Jesus; and angels came and
helped him.

Jesus Begins His Work in Galilee
(Mark 1.14–15; Luke 4.14–15)

12 When Jesus heard that John had been put in
prison, he went away to Galilee. 13 He did not stay
in Nazareth, but went to live in Capernaum, a town
by Lake Galilee, in the territory of Zebulun and
Naphtali. 14 This was done to make what the prophet
Isaiah had said come true,

15 "Land of Zebulun and land of Naphtali,
    on the road to the sea, on the other side of
        the Jordan,
    Galilee, land of the Gentiles!
16 The people who live in darkness
    will see a great light.
On those who live in the dark land of death
    the light will shine."

17 From that time Jesus began to preach his message: "Turn away from your sins, because the Kingdom
of heaven is near!"

Jesus Calls Four Fishermen
(Mark 1.16–20; Luke 5.1–11)

18 As Jesus walked along the shore of Lake Galilee,
he saw two brothers who were fishermen, Simon
(called Peter) and his brother Andrew, catching fish
in the lake with a net. 19 Jesus said to them, "Come
with me, and I will teach you to catch men." 20 At
once they left their nets and went with him.

21 He went on and saw two other brothers, James

and John, the sons of Zebedee. They were in their boat with their father Zebedee, getting their nets ready. Jesus called them, 22 and at once they left the boat and their father, and went with him.

Jesus Teaches, Preaches, and Heals
(Luke 6.17–19)

23 Jesus went all over Galilee, teaching in the synagogues, preaching the Good News about the Kingdom, and healing people who had all kinds of disease and sickness. 24 The news about him spread through the whole country of Syria, so that people brought to him all those who were sick, suffering from all kinds of diseases and disorders: people with demons, and epileptics, and paralytics—and Jesus healed them all. 25 Large crowds followed him from Galilee and the Ten Towns, from Jerusalem, Judaea, and the land on the other side of the Jordan.

The Sermon on the Mount

5 Jesus saw the crowds and went up a hill, where he sat down. His disciples gathered round him, 2 and he began to teach them:

True Happiness
(Luke 6.20–23)

3 "Happy are those who know they are spiritually
    poor;
  the Kingdom of heaven belongs to them!
4 "Happy are those who mourn;
  God will comfort them!
5 "Happy are those who are humble;
  they will receive what God has promised!
6 "Happy are those whose greatest desire is to do
    what God requires;
  God will satisfy them fully!
7 "Happy are those who are merciful to others;
  God will be merciful to them!
8 "Happy are the pure in heart;
  they will see God!
9 "Happy are those who work for peace;
  God will call them his children!

10 "Happy are those who are persecuted because they
    do what God requires;
    the Kingdom of heaven belongs to them!

11 "Happy are you when people insult you and persecute you and tell all kinds of evil lies against you
because you are my followers. 12 Be happy and glad,
for a great reward is kept for you in heaven. This
is how the prophets who lived before you were persecuted.

Salt and Light
(Mark 9.50; Luke 14.34–35)

13 "You are like salt for all mankind. But if salt
loses its saltiness, there is no way to make it salty
again. It has become worthless, so it is thrown out
and people trample on it.

14 "You are like light for the whole world. A city
built on a hill cannot be hidden. 15 No one lights a
lamp and puts it under a bowl; instead he puts it
on the lampstand, where it gives light for everyone in
the house. 16 In the same way your light must shine
before people, so that they will see the good things
you do and praise your Father in heaven.

Teaching about the Law

17 "Do not think that I have come to do away
with the Law of Moses and the teachings of the
prophets. I have not come to do away with them,
but to make their teachings come true. 18 Remember
that as long as heaven and earth last, not the least
point nor the smallest detail of the Law will be done
away with—not until the end of all things.a 19 So
then, whoever disobeys even the least important of
the commandments and teaches others to do the same,
will be least in the Kingdom of heaven. On the other
hand, whoever obeys the Law and teaches others to
do the same, will be great in the Kingdom of heaven.
20 I tell you, then, that you will be able to enter
the Kingdom of heaven only if you are more faithful
than the teachers of the Law and the Pharisees in
doing what God requires.

a the end of all things; or all its teachings come true.

Teaching about Anger

21 "You have heard that people were told in the past, 'Do not commit murder; anyone who does will be brought to trial.' 22But now I tell you: whoever is angry[b] with his brother will be brought to trial, whoever calls his brother 'You good-for-nothing!' will be brought before the Council, and whoever calls his brother a worthless fool will be in danger of going to the fire of hell. 23So if you are about to offer your gift to God at the altar and there you remember that your brother has something against you, 24leave your gift there in front of the altar, go at once and make peace with your brother, and then come back and offer your gift to God.

25 "If someone brings a lawsuit against you and takes you to court, settle the dispute with him while there is time, before you get to court. Once you are there, he will hand you over to the judge, who will hand you over to the police, and you will be put in jail. 26There you will stay, I tell you, until you pay the last penny of your fine.

Teaching about Adultery

27 "You have heard that it was said, 'Do not commit adultery.' 28But now I tell you: anyone who looks at a woman and wants to possess her is guilty of committing adultery with her in his heart. 29So if your right eye causes you to sin, take it out and throw it away! It is much better for you to lose a part of your body than to have your whole body thrown into hell. 30If your right hand causes you to sin, cut it off and throw it away! It is much better for you to lose one of your limbs than for your whole body to go to hell.

Teaching about Divorce
(Matt. 19.9; Mark 10.11-12; Luke 16.18)

31 "It was also said, 'Anyone who divorces his wife must give her a written notice of divorce.' 32But now

[b]whoever is angry; *some manuscripts have* whoever without cause is angry.

I tell you: if a man divorces his wife, even though she has not been unfaithful, then he is guilty of making her commit adultery if she marries again; and the man who marries her commits adultery also.

Teaching about Vows

33 "You have also heard that people were told in the past, 'Do not break your promise, but do what you have vowed to the Lord to do.' 34But now I tell you: do not use any vow when you make a promise. Do not swear by heaven, because it is God's throne; 35nor by earth, because it is the resting place for his feet; not by Jerusalem, because it is the city of the great King. 36Do not even swear by your head, because you cannot make a single hair white or black. 37Just say 'Yes' or 'No'—anything else you say comes from the Evil One.

Teaching about Revenge
(Luke 6.29-30)

38 "You have heard that it was said, 'An eye for an eye, and a tooth for a tooth.' 39But now I tell you: do not take revenge on someone who wrongs you. If anyone slaps you on the right cheek, let him slap your left cheek too. 40And if someone takes you to court to sue you for your shirt, let him have your coat as well. 41And if one of the occupation troops forces you to carry his pack one kilometre, carry it two kilometres. 42When someone asks you for something, give it to him; when someone wants to borrow something, lend it to him.

Love for Enemies
(Luke 6.27-28, 32-36)

43 "You have heard that it was said, 'Love your friends, hate your enemies.' 44But now I tell you: love your enemies and pray for those who persecute you, 45so that you may become the sons of your Father in heaven. For he makes his sun to shine on bad and good people alike, and gives rain to those who do good and to those who do evil. 46Why should God reward you if you love only the people who love you? Even the tax collectors do that! 47And

if you speak only to your friends, have you done anything out of the ordinary? Even the pagans do that! ⁴⁸You must be perfect—just as your Father in heaven is perfect!

Teaching about Charity

6 "Make certain you do not perform your religious duties in public so that people will see what you do. If you do these things publicly, you will not have any reward from your Father in heaven.

2 "So when you give something to a needy person,

Do not make a big show of it (6.2)

do not make a big show of it, as the hypocrites do in the houses of worship and on the streets. They do it so that people will praise them. I assure you, they have already been paid in full. ³But when you help a needy person, do it in such a way that even your closest friend will not know about it. ⁴Then it will be a private matter. And your Father, who sees what you do in private, will reward you.

Teaching about Prayer
(Luke 11.2–4)

5 "When you pray, do not be like the hypocrites!
They love to stand up and pray in the houses of
worship and on the street corners, so that everyone
will see them. I assure you, they have already been paid
in full. 6But when you pray, go to your room, close
the door, and pray to your Father, who is unseen.
And your Father, who sees what you do in private,
will reward you.

7 "When you pray, do not use a lot of meaningless
words, as the pagans do, who think that God will
hear them because their prayers are long. 8Do not
be like them. Your Father already knows what you
need before you ask him. 9This, then, is how you
should pray:
  'Our Father in heaven:
    May your holy name be honoured;
10   may your Kingdom come;
    may your will be done on earth as it is in heaven.
11   Give us today the food we need. c
12   Forgive us the wrongs we have done,
    as we forgive the wrongs that others have done
      to us.
13   Do not bring us to hard testing,
    but keep us safe from the Evil One.'

14 "If you forgive others the wrongs they have done
to you, your Father in heaven will also forgive you.
15But if you do not forgive others, then your Father
will not forgive the wrongs you have done.

Teaching about Fasting

16 "And when you fast, do not put on a sad face
as the hypocrites do. They neglect their appearance
so that everyone will see that they are fasting. I
assure you, they have already been paid in full. 17When
you go without food, wash your face and comb your
hair, 18so that others cannot know that you are fasting—only your Father, who is unseen, will know. And

cwe need; or for today; or for tomorrow.

your Father, who sees what you do in private, will reward you.

Riches in Heaven
(Luke 12.33–34)

19 "Do not store up riches for yourselves here on earth, where moths and rust destroy; and robbers break in and steal. 20 Instead, store up riches for yourselves in heaven, where moths and rust cannot destroy, and robbers cannot break in and steal. 21 For your heart will always be where your riches are.

The Light of the Body
(Luke 11.34–36)

22 "The eyes are like a lamp for the body. If your eyes are sound, your whole body will be full of light; 23 but if your eyes are no good, your body will be in darkness. So if the light in you is darkness, how terribly dark it will be!

God and Possessions
(Luke 16.13; 12.22–31)

24 "No one can be a slave of two masters; he will hate one and love the other; he will be loyal to one and despise the other. You cannot serve both God and money.

25 "This is why I tell you not to be worried about the food and drink you need in order to stay alive, or about clothes for your body. After all, isn't life worth more than food? And isn't the body worth more than clothes? 26 Look at the birds flying around: they do not sow seeds, gather a harvest and put it in barns; yet your Father in heaven takes care of them! Aren't you worth much more than birds? 27 Can any of you live a bit longer[d] by worrying about it?

28 "And why worry about clothes? Look how the wild flowers grow: they do not work or make clothes for themselves. 29 But I tell you that not even King Solomon with all his wealth had clothes as beautiful as one of these flowers. 30 It is God who clothes the

[d] live a bit longer; or grow a bit taller.

Aren't you worth much more than birds? (6.26)

wild grass—grass that is here today and gone tomorrow, burnt up in the oven. Won't he be all the more sure to clothe you? How little faith you have!

31 "So do not start worrying: 'Where will my food come from? or my drink? or my clothes?' 32 (These are the things the pagans are always concerned about.) Your Father in heaven knows that you need all these things. 33 Instead, be concerned above everything else with the Kingdom of God and with what he requires of you, and he will provide you with all these other things. 34 So do not worry about tomorrow; it will have enough worries of its own. There is no need to add to the troubles each day brings.

Judging Others
(Luke 6.37–38, 41–42)

7 "Do not judge others, so that God will not judge you, 2 for God will judge you in the same way as you judge others, and he will apply to you the same rules you apply to others. 3 Why, then, do you look at the speck in your brother's eye, and pay no attention to the log in your own eye? 4 How dare you say to your brother, 'Please, let me take that

speck out of your eye,' when you have a log in your own eye? ⁵You hypocrite! First take the log out of your own eye, and then you will be able to see clearly to take the speck out of your brother's eye.

6 "Do not give what is holy to dogs—they will only turn and attack you. Do not throw your pearls in front of pigs—they will only trample them underfoot.

Ask, Seek, Knock
(Luke 11.9-13)

7 "Ask, and you will receive; seek, and you will find; knock, and the door will be opened to you. ⁸For everyone who asks will receive, and anyone who seeks will find, and the door will be opened to him who knocks. ⁹Would any of you who are fathers give your son a stone when he asks for bread? ¹⁰Or would you give him a snake when he asks for a fish? ¹¹Bad as you are, you know how to give good things to your children. How much more, then, will your Father in heaven give good things to those who ask him!

12 "Do for others what you want them to do for you: this is the meaning of the Law of Moses and of the teachings of the prophets.

The Narrow Gate
(Luke 13.24)

13 "Go in through the narrow gate, because the gate to hell is wide and the road that leads to it is easy, and there are many who travel it. ¹⁴But the gate to life is narrow and the way that leads to it is hard, and there are few people who find it.

A Tree and Its Fruit
(Luke 6.43-44)

15 "Be on your guard against false prophets; they come to you looking like sheep on the outside, but on the inside they are really like wild wolves. ¹⁶You will know them by what they do. Thorn bushes do not bear grapes, and briars do not bear figs. ¹⁷A healthy tree bears good fruit, but a poor tree bears

bad fruit. ¹⁸A healthy tree cannot bear bad fruit, and a poor tree cannot bear good fruit. ¹⁹And any tree that does not bear good fruit is cut down and thrown in the fire. ²⁰So then, you will know the false prophets by what they do.

I Never Knew You
(Luke 13.25-27)

21 "Not everyone who calls me 'Lord, Lord' will enter the Kingdom of heaven, but only those who do what my Father in heaven wants them to do. ²²When Judgement Day comes, many will say to me, 'Lord, Lord! In your name we spoke God's message, by your name we drove out many demons and performed many miracles!' ²³Then I will say to them, 'I never knew you. Get away from me, you wicked people!'

The Two House Builders
(Luke 6.47-49)

24 "So then, anyone who hears these words of mine and obeys them is like a wise man who built his house on rock. ²⁵The rain poured down, the rivers overflowed, and the wind blew hard against that house. But it did not fall, because it was built on rock.

26 "But anyone who hears these words of mine and does not obey them is like a foolish man who built his house on sand. ²⁷The rain poured down, the rivers overflowed, the wind blew hard against that house, and it fell. And what a terrible fall that was!"

The Authority of Jesus

28 When Jesus finished saying these things, the crowd was amazed at the way he taught. ²⁹He wasn't like the teachers of the Law; instead, he taught with authority.

Jesus Heals a Man
(Mark 1.40-45; Luke 5.12-16)

8 When Jesus came down from the hill, large crowds followed him. ²Then a man suffering from a dreaded skin-disease came to him, knelt down before

him, and said, "Sir, if you want to, you can make me clean." [e]

3 Jesus stretched out his hand and touched him. "I do want to," he answered. "Be clean!" At once the man was healed of his disease. [4]Then Jesus said to him, "Listen! Don't tell anyone, but go straight to the priest and let him examine you; then in order to prove to everyone that you are cured, offer the sacrifice that Moses ordered."

Jesus Heals a Roman Officer's Servant
(Luke 7.1–10)

5 When Jesus entered Capernaum, a Roman officer met him and begged for help: [6]"Sir, my servant is sick in bed at home, unable to move and suffering terribly."

7 "I will go and make him well," Jesus said.

8 "Oh no, sir," answered the officer. "I do not deserve to have you come into my house. Just give the order, and my servant will get well. [9]I, too, am a man under the authority of superior officers, and I have soldiers under me. I order this one, 'Go!' and he goes; and I order that one, 'Come!' and he comes; and I order my slave, 'Do this!' and he does it."

10 When Jesus heard this, he was surprised and said to the people following him, "I tell you, I have never found anyone in Israel with faith like this. [11]I assure you that many will come from the east and the west and sit down with Abraham, Isaac, and Jacob at the feast in the Kingdom of heaven. [12]But those who should be in the Kingdom will be thrown out into the darkness, where they will cry and grind their teeth." [13]Then Jesus said to the officer, "Go home, and what you believe will be done for you."

And the officer's servant was healed that very moment.

Jesus Heals Many People
(Mark 1.29–34; Luke 4.38–41)

14 Jesus went to Peter's home, and there he saw

[e]MAKE ME CLEAN: *This disease was considered to make a person ritually unclean.*

Peter's mother-in-law sick in bed with a fever. 15He touched her hand; the fever left her, and she got up and began to wait on him.

16 When evening came, people brought to Jesus many who had demons in them. Jesus drove out the evil spirits with a word and healed all who were sick. 17He did this to make what the prophet Isaiah had said come true, "He himself took our sickness and carried away our diseases."

The Would-be Followers of Jesus
(Luke 9.57–62)

18 When Jesus noticed the crowd round him, he ordered his disciples to go to the other side of the lake. 19A teacher of the Law came to him. "Teacher," he said, "I am ready to go with you wherever you go."

20 Jesus answered him, "Foxes have holes, and birds have nests, but the Son of Man has nowhere to lie down and rest."

21 Another man, who was a disciple, said, "Sir, first let me go back and bury my father."

22 "Follow me," Jesus answered, "and let the dead bury their own dead."

Jesus Calms a Storm
(Mark 4.35–41; Luke 8.22–25)

23 Jesus got into a boat, and his disciples went with him. 24Suddenly a fierce storm hit the lake, and the boat was in danger of sinking. But Jesus was asleep. 25The disciples went to him and woke him up. "Save us, Lord!" they said. "We are about to die!"

26 "Why are you so frightened?" Jesus answered. "How little faith you have!" Then he got up and ordered the winds and the waves to stop, and there was a great calm.

27 Everyone was amazed. "What kind of man is this?" they said. "Even the winds and the waves obey him!"

Jesus Heals Two Men with Demons
(Mark 5.1–20; Luke 8.26–39)

28 When Jesus came to the territory of Gadara on the other side of the lake, he was met by two men who came out of the burial caves there. These men had demons in them and were so fierce that no one dared travel on that road. 29 At once they screamed, "What do you want with us, you Son of God? Have you come to punish us before the right time?"

30 Not far away there was a large herd of pigs feeding. 31 So the demons begged Jesus, "If you are going to drive us out, send us into that herd of pigs."

32 "Go," Jesus told them; so they left and went off into the pigs. The whole herd rushed down the side of the cliff into the lake and was drowned.

33 The men who had been taking care of the pigs ran away and went into the town, where they told the whole story and what had happened to the men with the demons. 34 So everyone from the town went out to meet Jesus; and when they saw him, they begged him to leave their territory.

Jesus Heals a Paralysed Man
(Mark 2.1–12; Luke 5.17–26)

9 Jesus got into the boat and went back across the lake to his own town,f 2 where some people brought to him a paralysed man, lying on a bed. When Jesus saw how much faith they had, he said to the paralysed man, "Courage, my son! Your sins are forgiven."

3 Then some teachers of the Law said to themselves, "This man is speaking blasphemy!"

4 Jesus perceived what they were thinking, so he said, "Why are you thinking such evil things? 5 Is it easier to say, 'Your sins are forgiven,' or to say, 'Get up and walk'? 6 I will prove to you, then, that the Son of Man has authority on earth to forgive sins." So he said to the paralysed man, "Get up, pick up your bed, and go home!"

7 The man got up and went home. 8 When the people

fHIS OWN TOWN: *Capernaum (see 4.13).*

saw it, they were afraid, and praised God for giving
such authority to men.

Jesus Calls Matthew
(Mark 2.13–17; Luke 5.27–32)

9 Jesus left that place, and as he walked along,
he saw a tax collector, named Matthew, sitting in
his office. He said to him, "Follow me."

Matthew got up and followed him.

10 While Jesus was having a meal in Matthew's
house,g many tax collectors and other outcasts came
and joined Jesus and his disciples at the table. 11 Some
Pharisees saw this and asked his disciples, "Why does
your teacher eat with such people?"

12 Jesus heard them and answered, "People who
are well do not need a doctor, but only those who
are sick. 13 Go and find out what is meant by the
scripture that says: 'It is kindness that I want, not
animal sacrifices.' I have not come to call respectable
people, but outcasts."

The Question about Fasting
(Mark 2.18–22; Luke 5.33–39)

14 Then the followers of John the Baptist came to
Jesus, asking, "Why is it that we and the Pharisees
fast often, but your disciples don't fast at all?"

15 Jesus answered, "Do you expect the guests at
a wedding party to be sad as long as the bridegroom
is with them? Of course not! But the day will come
when the bridegroom will be taken away from them,
and then they will fast.

16 "No one patches up an old coat with a piece
of new cloth, for the new patch will shrink and make
an even bigger hole in the coat. 17 Nor does anyone
pour new wine into used wineskins, for the skins
will burst, the wine will pour out, and the skins will
be ruined. Instead, new wine is poured into fresh
wineskins, and both will keep in good condition."

gin Matthew's house; or in his (that is, Jesus') house.

The Official's Daughter and the Woman
Who Touched Jesus' Cloak
(Mark 5.21–43; Luke 8.40–56)

18 While Jesus was saying this, a Jewish official came to him, knelt down before him, and said, "My daughter has just died; but come and place your hands on her, and she will live."

19 So Jesus got up and followed him, and his disciples went along with him.

20 A woman who had suffered from severe bleeding for twelve years came up behind Jesus and touched the edge of his cloak. ²¹She said to herself, "If I

If I only touch his cloak (9.21)

only touch his cloak, I will get well."

22 Jesus turned round and saw her, and said, "Courage, my daughter! Your faith has made you well." At that very moment the woman became well.

23 Then Jesus went into the official's house. When he saw the musicians for the funeral and the people all stirred up, ²⁴he said, "Get out, everybody! The little girl is not dead—she is only sleeping!" Then they all laughed at him. ²⁵But as soon as the people had been put out, Jesus went into the girl's room and took hold of her hand, and she got up. ²⁶The news about this spread all over that part of the country.

Jesus Heals Two Blind Men

27 Jesus left that place, and as he walked along, two blind men started following him. "Take pity on us, Son of David!" they shouted.

28 When Jesus had gone indoors, the two blind men came to him, and he asked them, "Do you believe that I can heal you?"

"Yes, sir!" they answered.

29 Then Jesus touched their eyes and said, "Let it happen, then, just as you believe!"—30 and their sight was restored. Jesus spoke sternly to them, "Don't tell this to anyone!"

31 But they left and spread the news about Jesus all over that part of the country.

Jesus Heals a Dumb Man

32 As the men were leaving, some people brought to Jesus a man who could not talk because he had a demon. 33 But as soon as the demon was driven out, the man started talking, and everyone was amazed. "We have never seen anything like this in Israel!" they exclaimed.

34 But the Pharisees said, "It is the chief of the demons who gives him the power to drive out demons."

Jesus Has Pity for the People

35 Jesus went round visiting all the towns and villages. He taught in the synagogues, preached the Good News about the Kingdom, and healed people with every kind of disease and sickness. 36 As he saw the crowds, his heart was filled with pity for them, because they were worried and helpless, like sheep without a shepherd. 37 So he said to his disciples, "The harvest is large, but there are few workers to gather it in. 38 Pray to the owner of the harvest that he will send out workers to gather in his harvest."

The Twelve Apostles
(Mark 3.13-19; Luke 6.12-16)

10 Jesus called his twelve disciples together and gave them authority to drive out evil spirits and to heal every disease and every sickness. 2 These

are the names of the twelve apostles: first, Simon
(called Peter) and his brother Andrew; James and
his brother John, the sons of Zebedee; 3Philip and
Bartholomew; Thomas and Matthew, the tax collector;
James son of Alphaeus, and Thaddaeus; 4Simon the
Patriot, and Judas Iscariot, who betrayed Jesus.

The Mission of the Twelve
(Mark 6.7–13; Luke 9.1–6)

5 These twelve men were sent out by Jesus with
the following instructions: "Do not go to any Gentile
territory or any Samaritan towns. 6Instead, you are
to go to those lost sheep, the people of Israel. 7Go
and preach, 'The Kingdom of heaven is near!' 8Heal
the sick, bring the dead back to life, heal those who
suffer from dreaded skin-diseases, and drive out
demons. You have received without paying, so give
without being paid. 9Do not carry any gold, silver,
or copper money in your pockets; 10do not carry
a beggar's bag for the journey or an extra shirt or shoes
or a stick. A worker should be given what he needs.

11 "When you come to a town or village, go in
and look for someone who is willing to welcome you,
and stay with him until you leave that place. 12When
you go into a house, say, 'Peace be with you.' 13If the
people in that house welcome you, let your greeting
of peace remain; but if they do not welcome you,
then take back your greeting. 14And if some home
or town will not welcome you or listen to you, then
leave that place and shake the dust off your feet.
15I assure you that on the Judgement Day God will
show more mercy to the people of Sodom and
Gomorrah than to the people of that town!

Coming Persecutions
(Mark 13.9–13; Luke 21.12–17)

16 "Listen! I am sending you out just like sheep
to a pack of wolves. You must be as cautious as
snakes and as gentle as doves. 17Watch out, for there
will be men who will arrest you and take you to
court, and they will whip you in the synagogues.
18For my sake you will be brought to trial before
rulers and kings, to tell the Good News to them

and to the Gentiles. ¹⁹When they bring you to trial,
do not worry about what you are going to say or
how you will say it; when the time comes, you will
be given what you will say. ²⁰For the words you
will speak will not be yours; they will come from
the Spirit of your Father speaking through you.

21 "Men will hand over their own brothers to be
put to death, and fathers will do the same to their
children; children will turn against their parents and
have them put to death. ²²Everyone will hate you
because of me. But whoever holds out to the end
will be saved. ²³When they persecute you in one town,
run away to another one. I assure you that you will
not finish your work in all the towns of Israel before
the Son of Man comes.

24 "No pupil is greater than his teacher; no slave
is greater than his master. ²⁵So a pupil should be
satisfied to become like his teacher, and a slave like
his master. If the head of the family is called Beelzebul,
the members of the family will be called even worse
names!

Whom to Fear
(Luke 12.2–7)

26 "So do not be afraid of people. Whatever is
now covered up will be uncovered, and every secret
will be made known. ²⁷What I am telling you in
the dark you must repeat in broad daylight, and what
you have heard in private you must announce from
the housetops. ²⁸Do not be afraid of those who kill
the body but cannot kill the soul; rather be afraid
of God, who can destroy both body and soul in hell.
²⁹For only a penny you can buy two sparrows, yet
not one sparrow falls to the ground without your
Father's consent. ³⁰As for you, even the hairs of your
head have all been counted. ³¹So do not be afraid;
you are worth much more than many sparrows!

Confessing and Rejecting Christ
(Luke 12.8–9)

32 "If anyone declares publicly that he belongs to
me, I will do the same for him before my Father

in heaven. 33But if anyone rejects me publicly, I will reject him before my Father in heaven.

Not Peace, but a Sword
(Luke 12.51–53; 14.26–27)

34 "Do not think that I have come to bring peace to the world. No, I did not come to bring peace, but a sword. 35I came to set sons against their fathers, daughters against their mothers, daughters-in-law against their mothers-in-law; 36a man's worst enemies will be the members of his own family.

37 "Whoever loves his father or mother more than me is not fit to be my disciple; whoever loves his son or daughter more than me is not fit to be my disciple. 38Whoever does not take up his cross and follow in my steps is not fit to be my disciple. 39Whoever tries to gain his own life will lose it; but whoever loses his life for my sake will gain it.

Rewards
(Mark 9.41)

40 "Whoever welcomes you welcomes me; and whoever welcomes me welcomes the one who sent me. 41Whoever welcomes God's messenger because he is God's messenger, will share in his reward. And whoever welcomes a good man because he is good, will share in his reward. 42You can be sure that whoever gives even a drink of cold water to one of the least of these my followers because he is my follower, will certainly receive a reward."

The Messengers from John the Baptist
(Luke 7.18–35)

11 When Jesus finished giving these instructions to his twelve disciples, he left that place and went off to teach and preach in the towns near there.

2 When John the Baptist heard in prison about the things that Christ was doing, he sent some of his disciples to him. 3"Tell us," they asked Jesus, "are you the one John said was going to come, or should we expect someone else?"

4 Jesus answered, "Go back and tell John what you are hearing and seeing: 5the blind can see, the

G.N.T.B.M.–B

lame can walk, those who suffer from dreaded skin-diseases are made clean,[h] the deaf hear, the dead are brought back to life, and the Good News is preached to the poor. [6]How happy are those who have no doubts about me!"

7 While John's disciples were leaving, Jesus spoke about him to the crowds: "When you went out to John in the desert, what did you expect to see? A blade of grass bending in the wind? [8]What did you go out to see? A man dressed up in fancy clothes? People who dress like that live in palaces! [9]Tell me, what did you go out to see? A prophet? Yes indeed, but you saw much more than a prophet. [10]For John is the one of whom the scripture says: 'God said, I will send my messenger ahead of you to open the way for you.' [11]I assure you that John the Baptist is greater than any man who has ever lived. But he who is least in the Kingdom of heaven is greater than John. [12]From the time John preached his message until this very day the Kingdom of heaven has suffered violent attacks,[i] and violent men try to seize it. [13]Until the time of John all the prophets and the Law of Moses spoke about the Kingdom; [14]and if you are willing to believe their message, John is Elijah, whose coming was predicted. [15]Listen, then, if you have ears!

16 "Now, to what can I compare the people of this day? They are like children sitting in the marketplace. One group shouts to the other, [17]'We played wedding music for you, but you wouldn't dance! We sang funeral songs, but you wouldn't cry!' [18]When John came, he fasted and drank no wine, and everyone said, 'He has a demon in him!' [19]When the Son of Man came, he ate and drank, and everyone said, 'Look at this man! He is a glutton and a drinker, a friend of tax collectors and other outcasts!' God's wisdom, however, is shown to be true by its results."

The Unbelieving Towns
(Luke 10.13–15)

20 The people in the towns where Jesus had per-

[h]MADE CLEAN: See 8.2.
[i]has suffered violent attacks; or has been coming violently.

Come to me, all of you who are tired (11.28)

formed most of his miracles did not turn from their sins, so he reproached those towns. 21 "How terrible it will be for you, Chorazin! How terrible for you too, Bethsaida! If the miracles which were performed in you had been performed in Tyre and Sidon, the people there would long ago have put on sackcloth and sprinkled ashes on themselves, to show that they had turned from their sins! 22 I assure you that on the Judgement Day God will show more mercy to the people of Tyre and Sidon than to you! 23 And as for you, Capernaum! Did you want to lift yourself up to heaven? You will be thrown down to hell! If the miracles which were performed in you had been performed in Sodom, it would still be in existence today! 24 You can be sure that on the Judgement Day God will show more mercy to Sodom than to you!"

Come to Me and Rest
(Luke 10.21–22)

25 At that time Jesus said, "Father, Lord of heaven and earth! I thank you because you have shown to the unlearned what you have hidden from the wise and learned. 26 Yes, Father, this was how you wanted it to happen.

27 "My Father has given me all things. No one knows the Son except the Father, and no one knows the Father except the Son and those to whom the Son chooses to reveal him.

28 "Come to me, all of you who are tired from

carrying heavy loads, and I will give you rest. 29Take
my yoke and put it on you, and learn from me,
because I am gentle and humble in spirit; and you
will find rest. 30For the yoke I will give you is easy,
and the load I will put on you is light."

The Question about the Sabbath
(Mark 2.23–28; Luke 6.1–5)

12 Not long afterwards Jesus was walking through
some cornfields on the Sabbath. His disciples
were hungry, so they began to pick ears of corn
and eat the grain. 2When the Pharisees saw this,
they said to Jesus, "Look, it is against our Law for
your disciples to do this on the Sabbath!"

3 Jesus answered, "Have you never read what David
did that time when he and his men were hungry?
4He went into the house of God, and he and his
men ate the bread offered to God, even though it
was against the Law for them to eat it—only the
priests were allowed to eat that bread. 5Or have you
not read in the Law of Moses that every Sabbath the
priests in the Temple actually break the Sabbath law,
yet they are not guilty? 6I tell you that there is
something here greater than the Temple. 7The scripture
says, 'It is kindness that I want, not animal sacrifices.'
If you really knew what this means, you would not
condemn people who are not guilty; 8for the Son
of Man is Lord of the Sabbath."

The Man with a Paralysed Hand
(Mark 3.1–6; Luke 6.6–11)

9 Jesus left that place and went to a synagogue,
10where there was a man who had a paralysed hand.
Some people were there who wanted to accuse Jesus
of doing wrong, so they asked him, "Is it against
our Law to heal on the Sabbath?"

11 Jesus answered, "What if one of you has a sheep
and it falls into a deep hole on the Sabbath? Will
he not take hold of it and lift it out? 12And a man
is worth much more than a sheep! So then, our
Law does allow us to help someone on the Sabbath."
13Then he said to the man with the paralysed hand,
"Stretch out your hand."

He stretched it out, and it became well again, just like the other one. ¹⁴Then the Pharisees left and made plans to kill Jesus.

God's Chosen Servant

15 When Jesus heard about the plot against him, he went away from that place; and large crowds followed him. He healed all those who were ill ¹⁶and gave them orders not to tell others about him. ¹⁷He did this so as to make what God had said through the prophet Isaiah come true:

¹⁸ "Here is my servant, whom I have chosen,
   the one I love, and with whom I am pleased.
I will send my Spirit upon him,
   and he will announce my judgement to the nations.
¹⁹ He will not argue or shout,
   or make loud speeches in the streets.
²⁰ He will be gentle to those who are weak,
   and kind to those who are helpless.
He will persist until he causes justice to triumph,
²¹ and on him all peoples will put their hope."

Jesus and Beelzebul
(Mark 3.20–30; Luke 11.14–23)

22 Then some people brought to Jesus a man who was blind and could not talk because he had a demon. Jesus healed the man, so that he was able to talk and see. ²³The crowds were all amazed at what Jesus had done. "Could he be the Son of David?" they asked.

24 When the Pharisees heard this, they replied, "He drives out demons only because their ruler Beelzebul gives him power to do so."

25 Jesus knew what they were thinking, so he said to them, "Any country that divides itself into groups which fight each other will not last very long. And any town or family that divides itself into groups which fight each other will fall apart. ²⁶So if one group is fighting another in Satan's kingdom, this means that it is already divided into groups and will soon fall apart! ²⁷You say that I drive out demons because Beelzebul gives me the power to do so. Well, then, who gives your followers the power to drive

them out? What your own followers do proves that you
are wrong! 28No, it is not Beelzebul, but God's Spirit,
who gives me the power to drive out demons, which
proves that the Kingdom of God has already come
upon you.

29 "No one can break into a strong man's house
and take away his belongings unless he first ties up
the strong man; then he can plunder his house.

30 "Anyone who is not for me is really against
me; anyone who does not help me gather is really
scattering. 31And so I tell you that people can be
forgiven any sin and any evil thing they say;*j* but
whoever says evil things against the Holy Spirit will
not be forgiven. 32Anyone who says something against
the Son of Man can be forgiven; but whoever says
something against the Holy Spirit will not be forgiven—
now or ever.

A Tree and Its Fruit
(Luke 6.43–45)

33 "To have good fruit you must have a healthy
tree; if you have a poor tree, you will have bad
fruit. A tree is known by the kind of fruit it bears.
34You snakes—how can you say good things when
you are evil? For the mouth speaks what the heart
is full of. 35A good person brings good things out
of his treasure of good things; a bad person brings
bad things out of his treasure of bad things.

36 "You can be sure that on Judgement Day everyone will have to give account of every useless word
he has ever spoken. 37Your words will be used to
judge you—to declare you either innocent or guilty."

The Demand for a Miracle
(Mark 8.11–12; Luke 11.29–32)

38 Then some teachers of the Law and some Pharisees spoke up. "Teacher," they said, "we want to
see you perform a miracle."

39 "How evil and godless are the people of this
day!" Jesus exclaimed. "You ask me for a miracle?
No! The only miracle you will be given is the miracle

j evil thing they say; *or* evil thing they say against God.

of the prophet Jonah. ⁴⁰In the same way that Jonah spent three days and nights in the big fish, so will the Son of Man spend three days and nights in the depths of the earth. ⁴¹On Judgement Day the people of Nineveh will stand up and accuse you, because they turned from their sins when they heard Jonah preach; and I tell you that there is something here greater than Jonah! ⁴²On Judgement Day the Queen of Sheba will stand up and accuse you, because she travelled all the way from her country to listen to King Solomon's wise teaching; and I assure you that there is something here greater than Solomon!

The Return of the Evil Spirit
(Luke 11.24-26)

43 "When an evil spirit goes out of a person, it travels over dry country looking for a place to rest. If it can't find one, ⁴⁴it says to itself, 'I will go back to my house.' So it goes back and finds the house empty, clean, and all tidy. ⁴⁵Then it goes out and brings along seven other spirits even worse than itself, and they come and live there. So when it is all over, that person is in a worse state than he was at the beginning. This is what will happen to the evil people of this day."

Jesus' Mother and Brothers
(Mark 3.31-35; Luke 8.19-21)

46 Jesus was still talking to the people when his mother and brothers arrived. They stood outside, asking to speak with him. ⁴⁷So one of the people there said to him, "Look, your mother and brothers are standing outside, and they want to speak with you."ᵏ

48 Jesus answered, "Who is my mother? Who are my brothers?" ⁴⁹Then he pointed to his disciples and said, "Look! Here are my mother and my brothers! ⁵⁰Whoever does what my Father in heaven wants him to do is my brother, my sister, and my mother."

ᵏSome manuscripts do not have verse 47.

The Parable of the Sower
(Mark 4.1–9; Luke 8.4–8)

13 That same day Jesus left the house and went to the lake-side, where he sat down to teach. ²The crowd that gathered round him was so large that he got into a boat and sat in it, while the crowd stood on the shore. ³He used parables to tell them many things.

"Once there was a man who went out to sow corn. ⁴As he scattered the seed in the field, some of it fell along the path, and the birds came and ate it up. ⁵Some of it fell on rocky ground, where there was little soil. The seeds soon sprouted, because the soil wasn't deep. ⁶But when the sun came up, it burnt the young plants; and because the roots had not grown deep enough, the plants soon dried up. ⁷Some of the seed fell among thorn bushes, which grew up and choked the plants. ⁸But some seeds fell in good soil, and the plants produced corn; some produced a hundred grains, others sixty, and others thirty."

9 And Jesus concluded, "Listen, then, if you have ears!"

The Purpose of the Parables
(Mark 4.10–12; Luke 8.9–10)

10 Then the disciples came to Jesus and asked him, "Why do you use parables when you talk to the people?"

11 Jesus answered, "The knowledge about the secrets of the Kingdom of heaven has been given to you, but not to them. ¹²For the person who has something will be given more, so that he will have more than enough; but the person who has nothing will have taken away from him even the little he has. ¹³The reason I use parables in talking to them is that they look, but do not see, and they listen, but do not hear or understand. ¹⁴So the prophecy of Isaiah applies to them:

'This people will listen and listen, but not understand;
    they will look and look, but not see,
¹⁵ because their minds are dull,

and they have stopped up their ears
and have closed their eyes.
Otherwise, their eyes would see,
their ears would hear,
their minds would understand,
and they would turn to me, says God,
and I would heal them.'

16 "As for you, how fortunate you are! Your eyes see and your ears hear. 17 I assure you that many prophets and many of God's people wanted very much to see what you see, but they could not, and to hear what you hear, but they did not.

Jesus Explains the Parable of the Sower
(Mark 4.13-20; Luke 8.11-15)

18 "Listen, then, and learn what the parable of the sower means. 19 Those who hear the message about the Kingdom but do not understand it are like the seeds that fell along the path. The Evil One comes and snatches away what was sown in them. 20 The seeds that fell on rocky ground stand for those who receive the message gladly as soon as they hear it. 21 But it does not sink deep into them, and they don't last long. So when trouble or persecution comes because of the message, they give up at once. 22 The seeds that fell among thorn bushes stand for those who hear the message; but the worries about this life and the love for riches choke the message, and they don't bear fruit. 23 And the seeds sown in the good soil stand for those who hear the message and understand it: they bear fruit, some as much as a hundred, others sixty, and others thirty."

The Parable of the Weeds

24 Jesus told them another parable: "The Kingdom of heaven is like this. A man sowed good seed in his field. 25 One night, when everyone was asleep, an enemy came and sowed weeds among the wheat and went away. 26 When the plants grew and the ears of corn began to form, then the weeds showed up. 27 The man's servants came to him and said, 'Sir, it was good seed you sowed in your field; where did the weeds come from?' 28 'It was some enemy who

did this,' he answered. 'Do you want us to go and pull up the weeds?' they asked him. 29'No,' he answered, 'because as you gather the weeds you might pull up some of the wheat along with them. 30Let the wheat and the weeds both grow together until harvest. Then I will tell the harvest workers to pull up the weeds first, tie them in bundles and burn them, and then to gather in the wheat and put it in my barn.' "

The Parable of the Mustard Seed
(Mark 4.30–32; Luke 13.18–19)

31 Jesus told them another parable: "The Kingdom of heaven is like this. A man takes a mustard seed and sows it in his field. 32It is the smallest of all seeds, but when it grows up, it is the biggest of all plants. It becomes a tree, so that birds come and make their nests in its branches."

The Parable of the Yeast
(Luke 13.20–21)

33 Jesus told them still another parable: "The Kingdom of heaven is like this. A woman takes some yeast and mixes it with forty litres of flour until the whole batch of dough rises."

Jesus' Use of Parables
(Mark 4.33–34)

34 Jesus used parables to tell all these things to the crowds; he would not say a thing to them without using a parable. 35He did this to make what the prophet had said come true,
"I will use parables when I speak to them;
I will tell them things unknown since the creation of the world."

Jesus Explains the Parable of the Weeds

36 When Jesus had left the crowd and gone indoors, his disciples came to him and said, "Tell us what the parable about the weeds in the field means."
37 Jesus answered, "The man who sowed the good seed is the Son of Man; 38the field is the world; the good seed is the people who belong to the King-

dom; the weeds are the people who belong to the Evil One; 39 and the enemy who sowed the weeds is the Devil. The harvest is the end of the age, and the harvest workers are angels. 40 Just as the weeds are gathered up and burnt in the fire, so the same thing will happen at the end of the age: 41 the Son of Man will send out his angels to gather up out of his Kingdom all those who cause people to sin and all others who do evil things, 42 and they will throw them into the fiery furnace, where they will cry and grind their teeth. 43 Then God's people will shine like the sun in their Father's Kingdom. Listen, then, if you have ears!

The Parable of the Hidden Treasure

44 "The Kingdom of heaven is like this. A man happens to find a treasure hidden in a field. He covers it up again, and is so happy that he goes and sells everything he has, and then goes back and buys that field.

The Parable of the Pearl

45 "Also, the Kingdom of heaven is like this. A man is looking for fine pearls, 46 and when he finds one that is unusually fine, he goes and sells everything he has, and buys that pearl.

The Parable of the Net

47 "Also, the Kingdom of heaven is like this. Some fishermen throw their net out in the lake and catch all kinds of fish. 48 When the net is full, they pull it to shore and sit down to divide the fish: the good ones go into their buckets, the worthless ones are thrown away. 49 It will be like this at the end of the age: the angels will go out and gather up the evil people from among the good 50 and will throw them into the fiery furnace, where they will cry and grind their teeth.

New Truths and Old

51 "Do you understand these things?" Jesus asked them.

"Yes," they answered.

52 So he replied, "This means, then, that every teacher of the Law who becomes a disciple in the Kingdom of heaven is like the owner of a house who takes new and old things out of his storeroom."

Jesus is Rejected at Nazareth
(Mark 6.1-6; Luke 4.16-30)

53 When Jesus finished telling these parables, he left that place 54 and went back to his home town. He taught in the synagogue, and those who heard him were amazed. "Where did he get such wisdom?" they asked. "And what about his miracles? 55 Isn't he the carpenter's son? Isn't Mary his mother, and aren't James, Joseph, Simon, and Judas his brothers? 56 Aren't all his sisters living here? Where did he get all this?" 57 And so they rejected him.

Jesus said to them, "A prophet is respected everywhere except in his home town and by his own family." 58 Because they did not have faith, he did not perform many miracles there.

The Death of John the Baptist
(Mark 6.14-29; Luke 9.7-9)

14 At that time Herod, the ruler of Galilee, heard about Jesus. 2 "He is really John the Baptist, who has come back to life," he told his officials. "That is why he has this power to perform miracles."

3 For Herod had earlier ordered John's arrest, and he had him chained and put in prison. He had done this because of Herodias, his brother Philip's wife. 4 For some time John the Baptist had told Herod, "It isn't right for you to be married to Herodias!" 5 Herod wanted to kill him, but he was afraid of the Jewish people, because they considered John to be a prophet.

6 On Herod's birthday the daughter of Herodias danced in front of the whole group. Herod was so pleased 7 that he promised her, "I swear that I will give you anything you ask for!"

8 At her mother's suggestion she asked him, "Give me here and now the head of John the Baptist on a dish!"

9 The king was sad, but because of the promise

he had made in front of all his guests he gave orders
that her wish be granted. ¹⁰So he had John beheaded
in prison. ¹¹The head was brought in on a dish and
given to the girl, who took it to her mother. ¹²John's
disciples came, carried away his body, and buried
it; then they went and told Jesus.

Jesus Feeds Five Thousand Men
(Mark 6.30–44; Luke 9.10–17; John 6.1–14)

13 When Jesus heard the news about John, he left
there in a boat and went to a lonely place by himself.
The people heard about it, so they left their towns
and followed him by land. ¹⁴Jesus got out of the boat,
and when he saw the large crowd, his heart was
filled with pity for them, and he healed those who
were ill.

15 That evening his disciples came to him and said,
"It is already very late, and this is a lonely place.
Send the people away and let them go to the villages
to buy food for themselves."

16 "They don't have to leave," answered Jesus. "You
yourselves give them something to eat!"

17 "All we have here are five loaves and two fish,"
they replied.

18 "Then bring them here to me," Jesus said. ¹⁹He
ordered the people to sit down on the grass; then
he took the five loaves and the two fish, looked up
to heaven, and gave thanks to God. He broke the
loaves and gave them to the disciples, and the disciples
gave them to the people. ²⁰Everyone ate and had
enough. Then the disciples took up twelve baskets
full of what was left over. ²¹The number of men
who ate was about five thousand, not counting the
women and children.

Jesus Walks on the Water
(Mark 6.45–52; John 6.15–21)

22 Then Jesus made the disciples get into the boat
and go on ahead to the other side of the lake, while
he sent the people away. ²³After sending the people
away, he went up a hill by himself to pray. When evening came, Jesus was there alone; ²⁴and by this time
the boat was far out in the lake, tossed about by

the waves, because the wind was blowing against it.

25 Between three and six o'clock in the morning Jesus came to the disciples, walking on the water. 26When they saw him walking on the water, they were terrified. "It's a ghost!" they said, and screamed with fear.

27 Jesus spoke to them at once. "Courage!" he said. "It is I. Don't be afraid!"

28 Then Peter spoke up. "Lord, if it is really you, order me to come out on the water to you."

29 "Come!" answered Jesus. So Peter got out of the boat and started walking on the water to Jesus. 30But when he noticed the strong wind, he was afraid and started to sink down in the water. "Save me, Lord!" he cried.

31 At once Jesus reached out and grabbed hold of him and said, "How little faith you have! Why did you doubt?"

32 They both got into the boat, and the wind died down. 33Then the disciples in the boat worshipped Jesus. "Truly you are the Son of God!" they exclaimed.

Jesus Heals the Sick in Gennesaret
(Mark 6.53–56)

34 They crossed the lake and came to land at Gennesaret, 35where the people recognized Jesus. So they sent for the sick people in all the surrounding country and brought them to Jesus. 36They begged him to let those who were ill at least touch the edge of his cloak; and all who touched it were made well.

The Teaching of the Ancestors
(Mark 7.1–13)

15 Then some Pharisees and teachers of the Law came from Jerusalem to Jesus and asked him, 2"Why is it that your disciples disobey the teaching handed down by our ancestors? They don't wash their hands in the proper way before they eat!"

3 Jesus answered, "And why do you disobey God's command and follow your own teaching? 4For God said, 'Respect your father and your mother,' and 'Whoever curses his father or his mother is to be put

to death.' 5But you teach that if a person has something he could use to help his father or mother, but says, 'This belongs to God,' 6he does not need to honour his father.¹ In this way you disregard God's command, in order to follow your own teaching. 7You hypocrites! How right Isaiah was when he prophesied about you!

8 'These people, says God, honour me with their words,
     but their heart is really far away from me.
9 It is no use for them to worship me,
     because they teach man-made rules as though they
         were my laws!' "

The Things That Make a Person Unclean
(Mark 7.14–23)

10 Then Jesus called the crowd to him and said to them, "Listen and understand! 11It is not what goes into a person's mouth that makes him ritually unclean; rather, what comes out of it makes him unclean."

12 Then the disciples came to him and said, "Do you know that the Pharisees had their feelings hurt by what you said?"

13 "Every plant which my Father in heaven did not plant will be pulled up," answered Jesus. 14"Don't worry about them! They are blind leaders of the blind; and when one blind man leads another, both fall into a ditch."

15 Peter spoke up, "Explain this saying to us."

16 Jesus said to them, "You are still no more intelligent than the others. 17Don't you understand? Anything that goes into a person's mouth goes into his stomach and then on out of his body. 18But the things that come out of the mouth come from the heart, and these are the things that make a person ritually unclean. 19For from his heart come the evil ideas which lead him to kill, commit adultery, and do other immoral things; to rob, lie, and slander others. 20These are the things that make a person unclean. But to eat without washing your hands as they say you should—this doesn't make a person unclean."

¹his father; *some manuscripts have* his father or mother.

They are blind leaders of the blind (15.14)

A Woman's Faith
(Mark 7.24–30)

21 Jesus left that place and went off to the territory near the cities of Tyre and Sidon. 22 A Canaanite woman who lived in that region came to him. "Son of David!" she cried out. "Have mercy on me! My daughter has a demon and is in a terrible condition."

23 But Jesus did not say a word to her. His disciples came to him and begged him, "Send her away! She is following us and making all this noise!"

24 Then Jesus replied, "I have been sent only to those lost sheep, the people of Israel."

25 At this the woman came and fell at his feet. "Help me, sir!" she said.

26 Jesus answered, "It isn't right to take the children's food and throw it to the dogs."

27 "That's true, sir," she answered; "but even the dogs eat the leftovers that fall from their masters' table."

28 So Jesus answered her, "You are a woman of

great faith! What you want will be done for you."
And at that very moment her daughter was healed.

Jesus Heals Many People

29 Jesus left there and went along by Lake Galilee.
He climbed a hill and sat down. 30 Large crowds came
to him, bringing with them the lame, the blind, the
crippled, the dumb, and many other sick people, whom
they placed at Jesus' feet; and he healed them. 31 The
people were amazed as they saw the dumb speaking,
the crippled made whole, the lame walking, and the
blind seeing; and they praised the God of Israel.

Jesus Feeds Four Thousand Men
(Mark 8.1–10)

32 Jesus called his disciples to him and said, "I
feel sorry for these people, because they have been
with me for three days and now have nothing to
eat. I don't want to send them away without feeding
them, for they might faint on their way home."
33 The disciples asked him, "Where will we find
enough food in this desert to feed this crowd?"
34 "How much bread have you?" Jesus asked.
"Seven loaves," they answered, "and a few small
fish."
35 So Jesus ordered the crowd to sit down on the
ground. 36 Then he took the seven loaves and the fish,
gave thanks to God, broke them, and gave them to
the disciples; and the disciples gave them to the people.
37 They all ate and had enough. Then the disciples
took up seven baskets full of pieces left over. 38 The
number of men who ate was four thousand, not counting the women and children.
39 Then Jesus sent the people away, got into a
boat, and went to the territory of Magadan.

The Demand for a Miracle
(Mark 8.11–13; Luke 12.54–56)

16 Some Pharisees and Sadducees who came to
Jesus wanted to trap him, so they asked him
to perform a miracle for them, to show that God
approved of him. 2 But Jesus answered, "When the
sun is setting, you say, 'We are going to have fine

weather, because the sky is red.' ³And early in the
morning you say, 'It is going to rain, because the
sky is red and dark.' You can predict the weather
by looking at the sky, but you cannot interpret the
signs concerning these times!ᵐ ⁴How evil and godless
are the people of this day! You ask me for a miracle?
No! The only miracle you will be given is the miracle
of Jonah."

So he left them and went away.

The Yeast of the Pharisees and Sadducees
(Mark 8.14–21)

5 When the disciples crossed over to the other side
of the lake, they forgot to take any bread. ⁶Jesus
said to them, "Take care; be on your guard against
the yeast of the Pharisees and Sadducees."

7 They started discussing among themselves, "He
says this because we didn't bring any bread."

8 Jesus knew what they were saying, so he asked
them, "Why are you discussing among yourselves
about not having any bread? How little faith you
have! ⁹Don't you understand yet? Don't you remember
when I broke the five loaves for the five thousand
men? How many baskets did you fill? ¹⁰And what
about the seven loaves for the four thousand men?
How many baskets did you fill? ¹¹How is it that
you don't understand that I was not talking to you
about bread? Guard yourselves from the yeast of the
Pharisees and Sadducees!"

12 Then the disciples understood that he was not
warning them to guard themselves from the yeast
used in bread but from the teaching of the Pharisees
and Sadducees.

Peter's Declaration about Jesus
(Mark 8.27–30; Luke 9.18–21)

13 Jesus went to the territory near the town of
Caesarea Philippi, where he asked his disciples, "Who
do people say the Son of Man is?"

14 "Some say John the Baptist," they answered.

ᵐ Some manuscripts do not have the words of Jesus in verses 2
and 3.

"Others say Elijah, while others say Jeremiah or some other prophet."

15 "What about you?" he asked them. "Who do you say I am?"

16 Simon Peter answered, "You are the Messiah, the Son of the living God."

17 "Good for you, Simon son of John!" answered Jesus. "For this truth did not come to you from any human being, but it was given to you directly by my Father in heaven. 18 And so I tell you, Peter: you are a rock, and on this rock foundation I will build my church, and not even death will ever be able to overcome it. 19 I will give you the keys of the Kingdom of heaven; what you prohibit on earth will be prohibited in heaven, and what you permit on earth will be permitted in heaven."

20 Then Jesus ordered his disciples not to tell anyone that he was the Messiah.

Jesus Speaks about His Suffering and Death
(Mark 8.31—9.1; Luke 9.22-27)

21 From that time on Jesus began to say plainly to his disciples, "I must go to Jerusalem and suffer much from the elders, the chief priests, and the teachers of the Law. I will be put to death, but three days later I will be raised to life."

22 Peter took him aside and began to rebuke him. "God forbid it, Lord!" he said. "That must never happen to you!"

23 Jesus turned around and said to Peter, "Get away from me, Satan! You are an obstacle in my way, because these thoughts of yours don't come from God, but from man."

24 Then Jesus said to his disciples, "If anyone wants to come with me, he must forget self, carry his cross, and follow me. 25 For whoever wants to save his own life will lose it; but whoever loses his life for my sake will find it. 26 Will a person gain anything if he wins the whole world but loses his life? Of course not! There is nothing he can give to regain his life. 27 For the Son of Man is about to come in the glory of his Father with his angels, and then he will repay everyone according to his deeds. 28 I assure you that

there are some here who will not die until they have seen the Son of Man come as King."

The Transfiguration
(Mark 9.2–13; Luke 9.28–36)

17 Six days later Jesus took with him Peter and the brothers James and John and led them up a high mountain where they were alone. 2 As they looked on, a change came over Jesus: his face was shining like the sun, and his clothes were dazzling white. 3 Then the three disciples saw Moses and Elijah talking with Jesus. 4 So Peter spoke up and said to Jesus, "Lord, how good it is that we are here! If you wish, I will make three tents here, one for you, one for Moses, and one for Elijah."

5 While he was talking, a shining cloud came over them, and a voice from the cloud said, "This is my own dear Son, with whom I am pleased—listen to him!"

6 When the disciples heard the voice, they were so terrified that they threw themselves face downwards on the ground. 7 Jesus came to them and touched them. "Get up," he said. "Don't be afraid!" 8 So they looked up and saw no one there but Jesus.

9 As they came down the mountain, Jesus ordered them, "Don't tell anyone about this vision you have seen until the Son of Man has been raised from death."

10 Then the disciples asked Jesus, "Why do the teachers of the Law say that Elijah has to come first?"

11 "Elijah is indeed coming first," answered Jesus, "and he will get everything ready. 12 But I tell you that Elijah has already come and people did not recognize him, but treated him just as they pleased. In the same way they will also ill-treat the Son of Man."

13 Then the disciples understood that he was talking to them about John the Baptist.

Jesus Heals a Boy with a Demon
(Mark 9.14–29; Luke 9.37–43a).

14 When they returned to the crowd, a man came to Jesus, knelt before him, 15 and said, "Sir, have mercy on my son! He is an epileptic and has such terrible

fits that he often falls in the fire or into water. 16I brought him to your disciples, but they could not heal him."

17 Jesus answered, "How unbelieving and wrong you people are! How long must I stay with you? How long do I have to put up with you? Bring the boy here to me!" 18 Jesus gave a command to the demon, and it went out of the boy, and at that very moment he was healed.

19 Then the disciples came to Jesus in private and asked him, "Why couldn't we drive the demon out?"

20 "It was because you haven't enough faith," answered Jesus. "I assure you that if you have faith as big as a mustard seed, you can say to this hill, 'Go from here to there!' and it will go. You could do anything!"[n]

Jesus Speaks Again about His Death
(Mark 9.30–32; Luke 9.43b–45)

22 When the disciples all came together in Galilee, Jesus said to them, "The Son of Man is about to be handed over to men 23 who will kill him; but three days later he will be raised to life."

The disciples became very sad.

Payment of the Temple-Tax

24 When Jesus and his disciples came to Capernaum, the collectors of the temple-tax came to Peter and asked, "Does your teacher pay the temple-tax?"

25 "Of course," Peter answered.

When Peter went into the house, Jesus spoke up first, "Simon, what is your opinion? Who pays duties or taxes to the kings of this world? The citizens of the country or the foreigners?"

26 "The foreigners," answered Peter.

"Well, then," replied Jesus, "that means that the citizens don't have to pay. 27 But we don't want to offend these people. So go to the lake and drop in a line. Pull up the first fish you hook, and in its mouth

[n] Some manuscripts add verse 21: But only prayer and fasting can drive this kind out; nothing else can (see Mk 9.29).

you will find a coin worth enough for my temple-tax and yours. Take it and pay them **our taxes.**"

Who Is the Greatest?
(Mark 9.33–37; Luke 9.46–48)

18 At that time the disciples came to Jesus, asking, "Who is the greatest in the Kingdom of heaven?"

2 So Jesus called a child, made him stand in front of them, 3and said, "I assure you that unless you

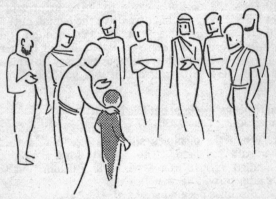

Unless you change and become like children (18.3)

change and become like children, you will never enter the Kingdom of heaven. 4The greatest in the Kingdom of heaven is the one who humbles himself and becomes like this child. 5And whoever welcomes in my name one such child as this, welcomes me.

Temptations to Sin
(Mark 9.42–48; Luke 17.1–2)

6 "If anyone should cause one of these little ones to lose his faith in me, it would be better for that person to have a large millstone tied round his neck and be drowned in the deep sea. 7How terrible for the world that there are things that make people lose their faith! Such things will always happen—but how terrible for the one who causes them!

8 "If your hand or your foot makes you lose your

faith, cut it off and throw it away! It is better for you to enter life without a hand or a foot than to keep both hands and both feet and be thrown into the eternal fire. ⁹And if your eye makes you lose your faith, take it out and throw it away! It is better for you to enter life with only one eye than to keep both eyes and be thrown into the fire of hell.

The Parable of the Lost Sheep
(Luke 15.3–7)

10 "See that you don't despise any of these little ones. Their angels in heaven, I tell you, are always in the presence of my Father in heaven. *o*

12 "What do you think a man does who has a

---

o Some manuscripts add verse 11: For the Son of Man came to save the lost *(see Lk 19.10)*.

He will...go and look for the lost sheep (18.12)

hundred sheep and one of them gets lost? He will
leave the other ninety-nine grazing on the hillside and
go and look for the lost sheep. 13 When he finds it,
I tell you, he feels far happier over this one sheep
than over the ninety-nine that did not get lost. 14 In
just the same way your[p] Father in heaven does not
want any of these little ones to be lost.

A Brother Who Sins

15 "If your brother sins against you,[q] go to him
and show him his fault. But do it privately, just
between yourselves. If he listens to you, you have
won your brother back. 16 But if he will not listen to
you, take one or two other persons with you, so
that 'every accusation may be upheld by the testimony
of two or more witnesses,' as the scripture says. 17 And
if he will not listen to them, then tell the whole
thing to the church. Finally, if he will not listen to
the church, treat him as though he were a pagan
or a tax collector.

Prohibiting and Permitting

18 "And so I tell all of you: what you prohibit
on earth will be prohibited in heaven, and what you
permit on earth will be permitted in heaven.

19 "And I tell you more: whenever two of you
on earth agree about anything you pray for, it will
be done for you by my Father in heaven. 20 For where
two or three come together in my name, I am there
with them."

The Parable of the Unforgiving Servant

21 Then Peter came to Jesus and asked, "Lord, if
my brother keeps on sinning against me, how many
times do I have to forgive him? Seven times?"

22 "No, not seven times," answered Jesus, "but
seventy times seven,[r] 23 because the Kingdom of heaven
is like this. Once there was a king who decided to
check on his servants' accounts. 24 He had just begun to

[p] your; *some manuscripts have* my.
[q] *Some manuscripts do not have* against you.
[r] seventy times seven; *or* seventy-seven times.

do so when one of them was brought in who owed him millions of pounds. 25 The servant did not have enough to pay his debt, so the king ordered him to be sold as a slave, with his wife and his children and all that he had, in order to pay the debt. 26 The servant fell on his knees before the king. 'Be patient with me,' he begged, 'and I will pay you everything!' 27 The king felt sorry for him, so he forgave him the debt and let him go.

28 "Then the man went out and met one of his fellow-servants who owed him a few pounds. He grabbed him and started choking him. 'Pay back what you owe me!' he said. 29 His fellow-servant fell down and begged him, 'Be patient with me, and I will pay you back!' 30 But he refused; instead, he had him thrown into jail until he should pay the debt. 31 When the other servants saw what had happened, they were very upset and went to the king and told him everything. 32 So he called the servant in. 'You worthless slave!' he said. 'I forgave you the whole amount you owed me, just because you asked me to. 33 You should have had mercy on your fellow-servant, just as I had mercy on you.' 34 The king was very angry, and he sent the servant to jail to be punished until he should pay back the whole amount."

35 And Jesus concluded, "That is how my Father in heaven will treat every one of you unless you forgive your brother from your heart."

Jesus Teaches About Divorce
(Mark 10.1–12)

19 When Jesus finished saying these things, he left Galilee and went to the territory of Judaea on the other side of the River Jordan. 2 Large crowds followed him, and he healed them there.

3 Some Pharisees came to him and tried to trap him by asking, "Does our Law allow a man to divorce his wife for whatever reason he wishes?"

4 Jesus answered, "Haven't you read the scripture that says that in the beginning the Creator made people male and female? 5 And God said, 'For this reason a man will leave his father and mother and unite with his wife, and the two will become one.'

⁶So they are no longer two, but one. Man must not separate, then, what God has joined together."

7 The Pharisees asked him, "Why, then, did Moses give the law for a man to hand his wife a divorce notice and send her away?"

8 Jesus answered, "Moses gave you permission to divorce your wives because you are so hard to teach. But it was not like that at the time of creation. ⁹I tell you, then, that any man who divorces his wife, even though she has not been unfaithful, commits adultery if he marries some other woman."

10 His disciples said to him, "If this is how it is between a man and his wife, it is better not to marry."

11 Jesus answered, "This teaching does not apply to everyone, but only to those to whom God has given it. ¹²For there are different reasons why men cannot marry: some, because they were born that way; others, because men made them that way; and others do not marry for the sake of the Kingdom of heaven. Let him who can accept this teaching do so."

Jesus Blesses Little Children
(Mark 10.13–16; Luke 18.15–17)

13 Some people brought children to Jesus for him to place his hands on them and to pray for them, but the disciples scolded the people. ¹⁴Jesus said, "Let the children come to me and do not stop them, because the Kingdom of heaven belongs to such as these."

15 He placed his hands on them and then went away.

The Rich Young Man
(Mark 10.17–31; Luke 18.18–30)

16 Once a man came to Jesus. "Teacher," he asked, "what good thing must I do to receive eternal life?"

17 "Why do you ask me concerning what is good?" answered Jesus. "There is only One who is good. Keep the commandments if you want to enter life."

18 "What commandments?" he asked.

Jesus answered, "Do not commit murder; do not commit adultery; do not steal; do not accuse anyone falsely; [19]respect your father and your mother; and love your neighbour as you love yourself."

20 "I have obeyed all these commandments," the young man replied. "What else do I need to do?"

21 Jesus said to him, "If you want to be perfect, go and sell all you have and give the money to the poor, and you will have riches in heaven; then come and follow me."

22 When the young man heard this, he went away sad, because he was very rich.

23 Jesus then said to his disciples, "I assure you: it will be very hard for rich people to enter the Kingdom of heaven. [24]I repeat: it is much harder for a rich person to enter the Kingdom of God than for a camel to go through the eye of a needle."

25 When the disciples heard this, they were completely amazed. "Who, then, can be saved?" they asked.

26 Jesus looked straight at them and answered, "This is impossible for man, but for God everything is possible."

27 Then Peter spoke up. "Look," he said, "we have left everything and followed you. What will we have?"

28 Jesus said to them, "You can be sure that when the Son of Man sits on his glorious throne in the New Age, then you twelve followers of mine will also sit on thrones, to rule the twelve tribes of Israel. [29]And everyone who has left houses or brothers or sisters or father or mother or children or fields for my sake, will receive a hundred times more and will be given eternal life. [30]But many who now are first will be last, and many who now are last will be first.

The Workers in the Vineyard

20 "The Kingdom of heaven is like this. Once there was a man who went out early in the morning to hire some men to work in his vineyard. [2]He agreed to pay them the regular wage, a silver coin a day, and sent them to work in his vineyard. [3]He went out again to the market place at nine o'clock and saw some men standing there doing nothing, [4]so he told them, 'You also go and work in the vineyard, and I will pay you a fair wage.' [5]So they went. Then

at twelve o'clock and again at three o'clock he did
the same thing. 6It was nearly five o'clock when he
went to the market place and saw some other men
still standing there. 'Why are you wasting the whole
day here doing nothing?' he asked them. 7'No one
hired us,' they answered. 'Well, then, you also go
and work in the vineyard,' he told them.

8 "When evening came, the owner told his foreman,
'Call the workers and pay them their wages, starting
with those who were hired last and ending with those
who were hired first.' 9The men who had begun to
work at five o'clock were paid a silver coin each.
10So when the men who were the first to be hired
came to be paid, they thought they would get more;
but they too were given a silver coin each. 11They
took their money and started grumbling against the
employer. 12'These men who were hired last worked
only one hour,' they said, 'while we put up with a
whole day's work in the hot sun—yet you paid them
the same as you paid us!'

13 " 'Listen, friend,' the owner answered one of
them, 'I have not cheated you. After all, you agreed
to do a day's work for one silver coin. 14Now take
your pay and go home. I want to give this man
who was hired last as much as I have given you.
15Don't I have the right to do as I wish with my
own money? Or are you jealous because I am
generous?' "

16 And Jesus concluded, "So those who are last
will be first, and those who are first will be last."

Jesus Speaks a Third Time about His Death
(Mark 10.32-34; Luke 18.31-34)

17 As Jesus was going up to Jerusalem, he took
the twelve disciples aside and spoke to them privately,
as they walked along. 18"Listen," he told them, "we
are going up to Jerusalem, where the Son of Man
will be handed over to the chief priests and the teachers
of the Law. They will condemn him to death 19and
then hand him over to the Gentiles, who will mock
him, whip him, and crucify him; but three days later
he will be raised to life."

A Mother's Request
(Mark 10.35–45)

20 Then the wife of Zebedee came to Jesus with her two sons, bowed before him, and asked him a favour.

21 "What do you want?" Jesus asked her.

She answered, "Promise me that these two sons of mine will sit at your right and your left when you are King."

22 "You don't know what you are asking for," Jesus answered the sons. "Can you drink the cup of suffering that I am about to drink?"

"We can," they answered.

23 "You will indeed drink from my cup," Jesus told them, "but I do not have the right to choose who will sit at my right and my left. These places belong to those for whom my Father has prepared them."

24 When the other ten disciples heard about this, they became angry with the two brothers. 25 So Jesus called them all together and said, "You know that the rulers of the heathen have power over them, and the leaders have complete authority. 26 This, however, is not the way it shall be among you. If one of you wants to be great, he must be the servant of the rest; 27 and if one of you wants to be first, he must be your slave—28 like the Son of Man, who did not come to be served, but to serve and to give his life to redeem many people."

Jesus Heals Two Blind Men
(Mark 10.46–52; Luke 18.35–43)

29 As Jesus and his disciples were leaving Jericho, a large crowd was following. 30 Two blind men who were sitting by the road heard that Jesus was passing by, so they began to shout, "Son of David! Take pity on us!"

31 The crowd scolded them and told them to be quiet. But they shouted even more loudly, "Son of David! Take pity on us!"

32 Jesus stopped and called them. "What do you want me to do for you?" he asked them.

God bless him who comes in the name of the Lord! (21.9)

33 "Sir," they answered, "we want you to give us our sight!"

34 Jesus had pity on them and touched their eyes; at once they were able to see, and they followed him.

The Triumphant Entry into Jerusalem
(Mark 11.1–11; Luke 19.28–40; John 12.12–19)

21 As Jesus and his disciples approached Jerusalem, they came to Bethphage at the Mount of Olives. There Jesus sent two of the disciples on ahead 2with these instructions: "Go to the village there ahead of you, and at once you will find a donkey tied up with her colt beside her. Untie them and bring them to me. 3And if anyone says anything, tell him, 'The Master*s* needs them'; and then he will let them go at once."

4 This happened in order to make what the prophet had said come true:

5 "Tell the city of Zion,
 Look, your king is coming to you!
 He is humble and rides on a donkey
  and on a colt, the foal of a donkey."

6 So the disciples went and did what Jesus had told them to do: 7they brought the donkey and the colt, threw their cloaks over them, and Jesus got on. 8A large crowd of people spread their cloaks on the road while others cut branches from the trees and spread them on the road. 9The crowds walking in front of Jesus and those walking behind began to shout, "Praise to David's Son! God bless him who comes in the name of the Lord! Praise God!"

10 When Jesus entered Jerusalem, the whole city was thrown into an uproar. "Who is he?" the people asked.

11 "This is the prophet Jesus, from Nazareth in Galilee," the crowds answered.

Jesus Goes to the Temple
(Mark 11.15–19; Luke 19.45–48; John 2.13–22)

12 Jesus went into the Temple and drove out all

---

*s*The Master; or Their owner.

those who were buying and selling there. He overturned the tables of the money-changers and the stools of those who sold pigeons, 13 and said to them, "It is written in the Scriptures that God said, 'My Temple will be called a house of prayer.' But you are making it a hideout for thieves!"

14 The blind and the crippled came to him in the Temple, and he healed them. 15 The chief priests and the teachers of the Law became angry when they saw the wonderful things he was doing and the children shouting in the Temple, "Praise to David's Son!" 16 So they asked Jesus, "Do you hear what they are saying?"

"Indeed I do," answered Jesus. "Haven't you ever read this scripture? 'You have trained children and babies to offer perfect praise.' "

17 Jesus left them and went out of the city to Bethany, where he spent the night.

Jesus Curses the Fig-Tree
(Mark 11.12–14, 20–24)

18 On his way back to the city early next morning, Jesus was hungry. 19 He saw a fig-tree by the side of the road and went to it, but found nothing on it except leaves. So he said to the tree, "You will never again bear fruit!" At once the fig-tree dried up.

20 The disciples saw this and were astounded. "How did the fig-tree dry up so quickly?" they asked.

21 Jesus answered, "I assure you that if you believe and do not doubt, you will be able to do what I have done to this fig-tree. And not only this, but you will even be able to say to this hill, 'Get up and throw yourself in the sea,' and it will. 22 If you believe, you will receive whatever you ask for in prayer."

The Question about Jesus' Authority
(Mark 11.27–33; Luke 20.1–8)

23 Jesus came back to the Temple; and as he taught, the chief priests and the elders came to him and asked, "What right have you to do these things? Who gave you this right?"

24 Jesus answered them, "I will ask you just one question, and if you give me an answer, I will tell

you what right I have to do these things. 25 Where
did John's right to baptize come from: was it from God
or from man?"

They started to argue among themselves, "What
shall we say? If we answer, 'From God,' he will
say to us, 'Why, then, did you not believe John?'
26 But if we say, 'From man,' we are afraid of what
the people might do, because they are all convinced
that John was a prophet." 27 So they answered Jesus,
"We don't know."

And he said to them, "Neither will I tell you, then,
by what right I do these things.

The Parable of the Two Sons

28 "Now, what do you think? There was once a
man who had two sons. He went to the elder one
and said, 'Son, go and work in the vineyard today.'
29 'I don't want to,' he answered, but later he changed
his mind and went. 30 Then the father went to the
other son and said the same thing. 'Yes, sir,' he
answered, but he did not go. 31 Which one of the
two did what his father wanted?"

"The elder one," they answered.

So Jesus said to them, "I tell you: the tax collectors
and the prostitutes are going into the Kingdom of
God ahead of you. 32 For John the Baptist came to
you showing you the right path to take, and you
would not believe him; but the tax collectors and
the prostitutes believed him. Even when you saw this,
you did not later change your minds and believe him.

The Parable of the Tenants in the Vineyard
(Mark 12.1-12; Luke 20.9-19)

33 "Listen to another parable," Jesus said. "There
was once a landowner who planted a vineyard, put
a fence around it, dug a hole for the winepress, and
built a watch-tower. Then he let out the vineyard
to tenants and went on a journey. 34 When the time
came to gather the grapes, he sent his slaves to the
tenants to receive his share of the harvest. 35 The
tenants seized his slaves, beat one, killed another,
and stoned another. 36 Again the man sent other slaves,
more than the first time, and the tenants treated them

-the same way. 36Last of all he sent his son to them. 'Surely they will respect my son,' he said. 38But when the tenants saw the son, they said to themselves, 'This is the owner's son. Come on, let's kill him, and we will get his property!' 39So they seized him, threw him out of the vineyard, and killed him.

40 "Now, when the owner of the vineyard comes, what will he do to those tenants?" Jesus asked.

41 "He will certainly kill those evil men," they answered, "and let the vineyard out to other tenants, who will give him his share of the harvest at the right time."

42 Jesus said to them, "Haven't you ever read what the Scriptures say?

'The stone which the builders rejected as worthless
    turned out to be the most important of all.
This was done by the Lord;
    what a wonderful sight it is!'

43 "And so I tell you," added Jesus, "the Kingdom of God will be taken away from you and given to a people who will produce the proper fruits."*t*

45 The chief priests and the Pharisees heard Jesus' parables and knew that he was talking about them, 46so they tried to arrest him. But they were afraid of the crowds, who considered Jesus to be a prophet.

The Parable of the Wedding Feast
(Luke 14.15–24)

22 Jesus again used parables in talking to the people. 2"The Kingdom of heaven is like this. Once there was a king who prepared a wedding feast for his son. 3He sent his servants to tell the invited guests to come to the feast, but they did not want to come. 4So he sent other servants with this message for the guests: 'My feast is ready now; my bullocks and prize calves have been butchered, and everything is ready. Come to the wedding feast!' 5But the invited guests paid no attention and went about their business: one went to his farm, another to his shop, 6while

t Some manuscripts add verse 44: Whoever falls on this stone will be cut to pieces; and if the stone falls on someone, it will crush him to dust *(see Lk 20.18).*

others grabbed the servants, beat them, and killed them. 7 The king was very angry; so he sent his soldiers, who killed those murderers and burnt down their city 8 Then he called his servants and said to them, 'My wedding feast is ready, but the people I invited did not deserve it. 9 Now go to the main streets and invite to the feast as many people as you find.' 10 So the servants went out into the streets and gathered all the people they could find, good and bad alike; and the wedding hall was filled with people.

11 "The king went in to look at the guests and saw a man who was not wearing wedding clothes. 12 'Friend, how did you get in here without wedding clothes?' the king asked him. But the man said nothing. 13 Then the king told the servants, 'Tie him up hand and foot, and throw him outside in the dark. There he will cry and grind his teeth.' "

14 And Jesus concluded, "Many are invited, but few are chosen."

The Question about Paying Taxes
(Mark 12.13–17; Luke 20.20–26)

15 The Pharisees went off and made a plan to trap Jesus with questions. 16 Then they sent to him some of their disciples and some members of Herod's party. "Teacher," they said, "we know that you tell the truth. You teach the truth about God's will for man, without worrying about what people think, because you pay no attention to a man's status. 17 Tell us, then, what do you think? Is it against our Law to pay taxes to the Roman Emperor, or not?"

18 Jesus, however, was aware of their evil plan, and so he said, "You hypocrites! Why are you trying to trap me? 19 Show me the coin for paying the tax!"

They brought him the coin, 20 and he asked them, "Whose face and name are these?"

21 "The Emperor's," they answered.

So Jesus said to them, "Well, then, pay the Emperor what belongs to the Emperor, and pay God what belongs to God."

22 When they heard this, they were amazed; and they left him and went away.

The Question about Rising from Death
(Mark 12.18–27; Luke 20.27–40)

23 That same day some Sadducees came to Jesus
and claimed that people will not rise from death.
24"Teacher," they said, "Moses said that if a man
who has no children dies, his brother must marry
the widow so that they can have children who will
be considered the dead man's children. 25Now, there
were seven brothers who used to live here. The eldest
got married and died without having children, so he
left his widow to his brother. 26The same thing happened to the second brother, to the third, and finally
to all seven. 27Last of all, the woman died. 28Now,
on the day when the dead rise to life, whose wife will
she be? All of them had married her."

29 Jesus answered them, "How wrong you are! It
is because you don't know the Scriptures or God's
power. 30For when the dead rise to life, they will
be like the angels in heaven and will not marry.
31Now, as for the dead rising to life: haven't you
ever read what God has told you? He said, 32'I am
the God of Abraham, the God of Isaac, and the God
of Jacob.' He is the God of the living, not of the
dead."

33 When the crowds heard this, they were amazed
at his teaching.

The Great Commandment
(Mark 12.28–34; Luke 10.25–28)

34 When the Pharisees heard that Jesus had silenced
the Sadducees, they came together, 35and one of them,
a teacher of the Law, tried to trap him with a question.
36"Teacher," he asked, "which is the greatest commandment in the Law?"

37 Jesus answered, " 'Love the Lord your God with
all your heart, with all your soul, and with all your
mind.' 38This is the greatest and the most important
commandment. 39The second most important commandment is like it: 'Love your neighbour as you love
yourself.' 40The whole Law of Moses and the teachings
of the prophets depend on these two commandments."

The Question about the Messiah
(Mark 12.35–37; Luke 20.41–44)

41 When some Pharisees gathered together, Jesus asked them, 42"What do you think about the Messiah? Whose descendant is he?"

"He is David's descendant," they answered.

43 "Why, then," Jesus asked, "did the Spirit inspire David to call him 'Lord'? David said,

44 'The Lord said to my Lord:

Sit here on my right

until I put your enemies under your feet.'

45 If, then, David called him 'Lord,' how can the Messiah be David's descendant?"

46 No one was able to give Jesus any answer, and from that day on no one dared to ask him any more questions.

Jesus Warns against the Teachers of the Law and the Pharisees
(Mark 12.38–39; Luke 11.43, 46; 20.45–46)

23 Then Jesus spoke to the crowds and to his disciples. 2"The teachers of the Law and the Pharisees are the authorized interpreters of Moses' Law. 3So you must obey and follow everything they tell you to do; do not, however, imitate their actions, because they don't practise what they preach. 4They tie on to people's backs loads that are heavy and hard to carry, yet they aren't willing even to lift a finger to help them carry those loads. 5They do everything so that people will see them. Look at the straps with scripture verses on them which they wear on their foreheads and arms, and notice how large they are! Notice also how long are the tassels on their cloaks!u 6They love the best places at feasts and the reserved seats in the synagogues; 7they love to be greeted with respect in the market-places and to be called 'Teacher.' You must not be called 'Teacher', because you are all brothers of one another and have only one Teacher. 9And you must not call anyone here on

uTASSELS ON THEIR CLOAKS: *These tassels were worn as a sign of devotion to God (see Num 15.37-41).*

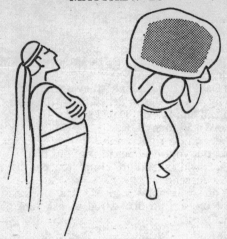

They aren't willing...to help them (23.4)

earth 'Father', because you have only the one Father in heaven. 10 Nor should you be called 'Leader', because your one and only leader is the Messiah. 11 The greatest one among you must be your servant. 12 Whoever makes himself great will be humbled, and whoever humbles himself will be made great.

Jesus Condemns Their Hypocrisy
(Mark 12.40; Luke 11.39–42, 44, 52; 20.47)

13 "How terrible for you, teachers of the Law and Pharisees! You hypocrites! You lock the door to the Kingdom of heaven in people's faces, and you yourselves don't go in, nor do you allow in those who are trying to enter! v

15 "How terrible for you, teachers of the Law and Pharisees! You hypocrites! You sail the seas and cross whole countries to win one convert; and when you

v Some manuscripts add verse 14: How terrible for you, teachers of the Law and Pharisees! You hypocrites! You take advantage of widows and rob them of their homes, and then make a show of saying long prayers! Because of this your punishment will be all the worse! (see Mk 12.40).

succeed, you make him twice as deserving of going
to hell as you yourselves are!

16 "How terrible for you, blind guides! You teach,

How terrible for you, blind guides! (23.16)

'If someone swears by the Temple, he isn't bound
by his vow; but if he swears by the gold in the
Temple, he is bound.' 17Blind fools! Which is more
important, the gold or the Temple which makes the
gold holy? 18You also teach, 'If someone swears by
the altar, he isn't bound by his vow; but if he swears
by the gift on the altar, he is bound.' 19How blind
you are! Which is the more important, the gift or
the altar which makes the gift holy? 20So then, when
a person swears by the altar, he is swearing by it
and by all the gifts on it; 21and when he swears
by the Temple, he is swearing by it and by God,
who lives there; 22and when someone swears by
heaven, he is swearing by God's throne and by him
who sits on it.

23 "How terrible for you, teachers of the Law and
Pharisees! You hypocrites! You give to God a tenth
even of the seasoning herbs, such as mint, dill, and
cumin, but you neglect to obey the really important
teachings of the Law, such as justice and mercy and
honesty. These you should practise, without neglecting

the others. 24Blind guides! You strain a fly out of
your drink, but swallow a camel!

25 "How terrible for you, teachers of the Law and
Pharisees! You hypocrites! You clean the outside of
your cup and plate, while the inside is full of what
you have obtained by violence and selfishness. 26Blind
Pharisee! Clean what is inside the cup first, and then
the outside will be clean too!

27 "How terrible for you, teachers of the Law and
Pharisees! You hypocrites! You are like whitewashed
tombs, which look fine on the outside but are full
of bones and decaying corpses on the inside. 28In
the same way, on the outside you appear good to
everybody, but inside you are full of hypocrisy and
sins.

Jesus Predicts Their Punishment
(Luke 11.47-51)

29 "How terrible for you, teachers of the Law and
Pharisees! You hypocrites! You make fine tombs for
the prophets and decorate the monuments of those
who lived good lives; 30and you claim that if you
had lived during the time of your ancestors, you would
not have done what they did and killed the prophets.
31So you actually admit that you are the descendants
of those who murdered the prophets! 32Go on, then,
and finish what your ancestors started! 33You snakes
and sons of snakes! How do you expect to escape
from being condemned to hell? 34And so I tell you
that I will send you prophets and wise men and
teachers; you will kill some of them, crucify others,
and whip others in the synagogues and chase them
from town to town. 35As a result, the punishment
for the murder of all innocent men will fall on you,
from the murder of innocent Abel to the murder of
Zachariah son of Berachiah, whom you murdered
between the Temple and the altar. 36I tell you indeed:
the punishment for all these murders will fall on the
people of this day!

Jesus' Love for Jerusalem
(Luke 13.34-35)

37 "Jerusalem, Jerusalem! You kill the prophets and

stone the messengers God has sent you! How many
times have I wanted to put my arms round all your
people, just as a hen gathers her chicks under her
wings, but you would not let me! [38]And so your
Temple will be abandoned and empty. [39]From now
on, I tell you, you will never see me again until
you say, 'God bless him who comes in the name
of the Lord.' "

Jesus Speaks of the Destruction of the Temple
(Mark 13.1-2; Luke 21.5-6)

24 Jesus left and was going away from the Temple
when his disciples came to him to call his attention to its buildings. [2]"Yes," he said, "you may well
look at all these. I tell you this: not a single stone here
will be left in its place; every one of them will be
thrown down."

Troubles and Persecutions
(Mark 13.3-13; Luke 21.7-19)

[3] As Jesus sat on the Mount of Olives, the disciples
came to him in private. "Tell us when all this will
be," they asked, "and what will happen to show that
it is the time for your coming and the end of the age."

[4] Jesus answered, "Be on your guard, and do not
let anyone deceive you. [5]Many men, claiming to speak
for me, will come and say, 'I am the Messiah!' and
they will deceive many people. [6]You are going to hear
the noise of battles close by and the news of battles
far away; but do not be troubled. Such things must
happen, but they do not mean that the end has come.
[7]Countries will fight each other, kingdoms will attack
one another. There will be famines and earthquakes
everywhere. [8]All these things are like the first pains
of childbirth.

[9] "Then you will be arrested and handed over to
be punished and be put to death. All mankind will
hate you because of me. [10]Many will give up their
faith at that time; they will betray one another and
hate one another. [11]Then many false prophets will
appear and deceive many people. [12]Such will be the
spread of evil that many people's love will grow cold.
[13]But whoever holds out to the end will be saved.

14And this Good News about the Kingdom will be preached through all the world for a witness to all mankind; and then the end will come.

The Awful Horror
(Mark 13.14–23; Luke 21.20–24)

15 "You will see 'The Awful Horror' of which the prophet Daniel spoke. It will be standing in the holy place." (Note to the reader: be sure to understand what this means!) 16"Then those who are in Judaea must run away to the hills. 17A man who is on the roof of his house must not take the time to go down and get his belongings from the house. 18A man who is in the field must not go back to get his cloak. 19How terrible it will be in those days for women who are pregnant and for mothers with little babies! 20Pray to God that you will not have to run away during the winter or on a Sabbath! 21For the trouble at that time will be far more terrible than any there has ever been, from the beginning of the world to this very day. Nor will there ever be anything like it again. 22But God has already reduced the number of days; had he not done so, nobody would survive. For the sake of his chosen people, however, God will reduce the days.

23 "Then, if anyone says to you, 'Look, here is the Messiah!' or 'There he is!'—do not believe him. 24For false Messiahs and false prophets will appear; they will perform great miracles and wonders in order to deceive even God's chosen people, if possible. 25Listen! I have told you this before the time comes.

26 "Or, if people should tell you, 'Look, he is out in the desert!'—don't go there; or if they say, 'Look, he is hiding here!'—don't believe it. 27For the Son of Man will come like the lightning which flashes across the whole sky from the east to the west.

28 "Wherever there is a dead body, the vultures will gather.

The Coming of the Son of Man
(Mark 13.24–27; Luke 21.25–28)

29 "Soon after the trouble of those days, the sun will grow dark, the moon will no longer shine, the

stars will fall from heaven, and the powers in space will be driven from their courses. 30 Then the sign of the Son of Man will appear in the sky; and all the peoples of earth will weep as they see the Son of Man coming on the clouds of heaven with power and great glory. 31 The great trumpet will sound, and he will send out his angels to the four corners of the earth, and they will gather his chosen people from one end of the world to the other.

The Lesson of the Fig-Tree
(Mark 13.28–31; Luke 21.29–33)

32 "Let the fig-tree teach you a lesson. When its branches become green and tender and it starts putting out leaves, you know that summer is near. 33 In the same way, when you see all these things, you will know that the time is near, ready to begin.w 34 Remember that all these things will happen before the people now living have all died. 35 Heaven and earth will pass away, but my words will never pass away.

No One Knows the Day and Hour
(Mark 13.32–37; Luke 17.26–30, 34–36)

36 "No one knows, however, when that day and hour will come—neither the angels in heaven nor the Son;x the Father alone knows. 37 The coming of the Son of Man will be like what happened in the time of Noah. 38 In the days before the flood people ate and drank, men and women married, up to the very day Noah went into the boat; 39 yet they did not realize what was happening until the flood came and swept them all away. That is how it will be when the Son of Man comes. 40 At that time two men will be working in a field: one will be taken away, the other will be left behind. 41 Two women will be at a mill grinding meal: one will be taken away, the other will be left behind.

42 "Be on your guard, then, because you do not know what day your Lord will come. 43 If the owner of a house knew the time when the thief would come,

wthe time is near, ready to begin; or he is near, ready to come.
xSome manuscripts do not have nor the Son.

you can be sure that he would stay awake and not let the thief break into his house. 44 So then, you also must always be ready, because the Son of Man will come at an hour when you are not expecting him.

The Faithful or the Unfaithful Servant
(Luke 12.41–48)

45 "Who, then, is a faithful and wise servant? He is the one that his master has placed in charge of the other servants to give them their food at the proper time. 46 How happy that servant is if his master finds him doing this when he comes home! 47 Indeed, I tell you, the master will put that servant in charge of all his property. 48 But if he is a bad servant, he will tell himself that his master will not come back for a long time, 49 and he will begin to beat his fellow-servants and to eat and drink with drunkards. 50 Then that servant's master will come back one day when the servant does not expect him and at a time he does not know. 51 The master will cut him in pieces*y* and make him share the fate of the hypocrites. There he will cry and grind his teeth.

The Parable of the Ten Girls

25 "At that time the Kingdom of heaven will be like this. Once there were ten girls who took their oil lamps and went out to meet the bridegroom. 2 Five of them were foolish, and the other five were wise. 3 The foolish ones took their lamps but did not take any extra oil with them, 4 while the wise ones took containers full of oil for their lamps. 5 The bridegroom was late in coming, so the girls began to nod and fall asleep.

6 "It was already midnight when the cry rang out, 'Here is the bridegroom! Come and meet him!' 7 The ten girls woke up and trimmed their lamps. 8 Then the foolish ones said to the wise ones, 'Let us have some of your oil, because our lamps are going out.' 9 'No, indeed,' the wise ones answered, 'there is not enough for you and for us. Go to the shop and buy some for yourselves.' 10 So the foolish girls went off

y cut him in pieces; *or* throw him out.

to buy some oil; and while they were gone, the bridegroom arrived. The five girls who were ready went in with him to the wedding feast, and the door was closed.

11 "Later the other girls arrived. 'Sir, sir! Let us in!' they cried out. 12'Certainly not! I don't know you,' the bridegroom answered."

13 And Jesus concluded, "Be on your guard, then, because you do not know the day or the hour.

The Parable of the Three Servants
(Luke 19.11–27)

14 "At that time the Kingdom of heaven will be like this. Once there was a man who was about to go on a journey; he called his servants and put them in charge of his property. 15He gave to each one according to his ability: to one he gave five thousand silver coins, to another he gave two thousand, and to another he gave one thousand. Then he left on his journey. 16The servant who had received five thousand coins went at once and invested his money and earned another five thousand. 17In the same way the servant who had received two thousand coins earned another two thousand. 18But the servant who had received one thousand coins went off, dug a hole in the ground, and hid his master's money.

19 "After a long time the master of those servants came back and settled accounts with them. 20The servant who had received five thousand coins came in and handed over the other five thousand. 'You gave me five thousand coins, sir,' he said. 'Look! Here are another five thousand that I have earned.' 21'Well done, you good and faithful servant!' said his master. 'You have been faithful in managing small amounts, so I will put you in charge of large amounts. Come on in and share my happiness!'

22 "Then the servant who had been given two thousand coins came in and said, 'You gave me two thousand coins, sir. Look! Here are another two thousand that I have earned.' 23'Well done, you good and faithful servant!' said his master. 'You have been faithful in managing small amounts, so I will put

you in charge of large amounts. Come on in and share my happiness!'

24 "Then the servant who had received one thousand coins came in and said, 'Sir, I know you are a hard man; you reap harvests where you did not sow, and you gather crops where you did not scatter seed. 25 I was afraid, so I went off and hid your money in the ground. Look! Here is what belongs to you.'

26 " 'You bad and lazy servant!' his master said. 'You knew, did you, that I reap harvests where I did not sow, and gather crops where I did not scatter seed? 27 Well, then, you should have deposited my money in the bank, and I would have received it all back with interest when I returned. 28 Now, take the money away from him and give it back to the one who has ten thousand coins. 29 For to every person who has something, even more will be given, and he will have more than enough; but the person who has nothing, even the little that he has will be taken away from him. 30 As for this useless servant—throw him outside in the darkness; there he will cry and grind his teeth.'

The Final Judgement

31 "When the Son of Man comes as King and all the angels with him, he will sit on his royal throne, 32 and the people of all the nations will be gathered before him. Then he will divide them into two groups, just as a shepherd separates the sheep from the goats. 33 He will put the righteous people on his right and the others on his left. 34 Then the King will say to the people on his right, 'Come, you that are blessed by my Father! Come and possess the kingdom which has been prepared for you ever since the creation of the world. 35 I was hungry and you fed me, thirsty and you gave me a drink; I was a stranger and you received me in your homes, 36 naked and you clothed me; I was sick and you took care of me, in prison and you visited me.'

37 "The righteous will then answer him, 'When, Lord, did we ever see you hungry and feed you, or thirsty and give you a drink? 38 When did we ever see you a stranger and welcome you in our

homes, or naked and clothe you? 39 When did we ever see you sick or in prison, and visit you?' 40 The King will reply, 'I tell you, whenever you did this for one of the least important of these brothers of mine, you did it for me!'

41 "Then he will say to those on his left, 'Away from me, you that are under God's curse! Away to the eternal fire which has been prepared for the Devil and his angels! 42 I was hungry but you would not feed me, thirsty but you would not give me a drink; 43 I was a stranger but you would not welcome me in your homes, naked but you would not clothe me; I was sick and in prison but you would not take care of me.'

44 "Then they will answer him, 'When, Lord, did we ever see you hungry or thirsty or a stranger or naked or sick or in prison, and would not help you?' 45 The King will reply, 'I tell you, whenever you refused to help one of these least important ones, you refused to help me.' 46 These, then, will be sent off to eternal punishment, but the righteous will go to eternal life."

The Plot against Jesus
(Mark 14.1–2; Luke 22.1–2; John 11.45–53)

26 When Jesus had finished teaching all these things, he said to his disciples, 2 "In two days, as you know, it will be the Passover Festival, and the Son of Man will be handed over to be crucified."

3 Then the chief priests and the elders met together in the palace of Caiaphas, the High Priest, 4 and made plans to arrest Jesus secretly and put him to death. 5 "We must not do it during the festival," they said, "or the people will riot."

Jesus Is Anointed at Bethany
(Mark 14.3–9; John 12.1–8)

6 Jesus was in Bethany at the house of Simon, a man who had suffered from a dreaded skin-disease. 7 While Jesus was eating, a woman came to him with an alabaster jar filled with an expensive perfume, which she poured on his head. 8 The disciples saw this and became angry. "Why all this waste?" they

asked. 9"This perfume could have been sold for a large amount and the money given to the poor!"

10 Jesus knew what they were saying, so he said to them, "Why are you bothering this woman? It is a fine and beautiful thing that she has done for me. 11You will always have poor people with you, but you will not always have me. 12What she did was to pour this perfume on my body to get me ready for burial. 13Now, I assure you that wherever this gospel is preached all over the world, what she has done will be told in memory of her."

Judas Agrees to Betray Jesus
(Mark 14.10–11; Luke 22.3–6)

14 Then one of the twelve disciples—the one named Judas Iscariot—went to the chief priests 15and asked,

Thirty silver coins (26.15)

"What will you give me if I betray Jesus to you?" They counted out thirty silver coins and gave them to him. 16From then on Judas was looking for a good chance to hand Jesus over to them.

Jesus Eats the Passover Meal with His Disciples
(Mark 14.12–21; Luke 22.7–14, 21–23; John 13.21–30)

17 On the first day of the Festival of Unleavened Bread the disciples came to Jesus and asked him, "Where do you want us to get the Passover meal ready for you?"

18 "Go to a certain man in the city," he said to them, "and tell him: 'The Teacher says, My hour has come; my disciples and I will celebrate the Passover at your house.' "

19 The disciples did as Jesus had told them and prepared the Passover meal.

20 When it was evening, Jesus and the twelve disciples sat down to eat. 21During the meal Jesus said, "I tell you, one of you will betray me."

22 The disciples were very upset and began to ask him, one after the other, "Surely, Lord, you don't mean me?"

23 Jesus answered, "One who dips his bread in the dish with me will betray me. 24The Son of Man will die as the Scriptures say he will, but how terrible for that man who betrays the Son of Man! It would have been better for that·man if he had never been born!"

25 Judas, the traitor, spoke up. "Surely, Teacher, you don't mean me?" he asked.

Jesus answered, "So you say."

The Lord's Supper
(Mark 14.22–26; Luke 22.14–20; 1 Cor. 11.23–25)

26 While they were eating, Jesus took a piece of bread, gave a prayer of thanks, broke it, and gave it to his disciples. "Take and eat it," he said; "this is my body."

27 Then he took a cup, gave thanks to God, and gave it to them. "Drink it, all of you," he said; 28"this is my blood, which seals God's covenant, my blood poured out for many for the forgiveness of sins. 29I tell you, I will never again drink this wine until the day I drink the new wine with you in my Father's Kingdom."

30 Then they sang a hymn and went out to the Mount of Olives.

Jesus Predicts Peter's Denial
(Mark 14.27–31; Luke 22.31–34; John 13.36–38)

31 Then Jesus said to them, "This very night all of·you will run away and leave me, for the scripture says, 'God will kill the shepherd, and the sheep of

the flock will be scattered.' ³²But after I am raised to
life, I will go to Galilee ahead of you."

33 Peter spoke up and said to Jesus, "I will never
leave you, even though all the rest do!"

34 Jesus said to Peter, "I tell you that before the
cock crows tonight, you will say three times that
you do not know me."

35 Peter answered, "I will never say that, even if
I have to die with you!"

And all the other disciples said the same thing.

Jesus Prays in Gethsemane
(Mark 14.32–42; Luke 22.39–46)

36 Then Jesus went with his disciples to a place
called Gethsemane, and he said to them, "Sit here
while I go over there and pray." ³⁷He took with
him Peter and the two sons of Zebedee. Grief and
anguish came over him, ³⁸and he said to them, "The
sorrow in my heart is so great that it almost crushes
me. Stay here and keep watch with me."

39 He went a little farther on, threw himself face

Take this cup of suffering from me! (26.39)

downwards on the ground, and prayed, "My Father,
if it is possible, take this cup of suffering from me!
Yet not what I want, but what you want."

40 Then he returned to the three disciples and found
them asleep; and he said to Peter, "How is it that
you three were not able to keep watch with me even
for one hour? ⁴¹Keep watch and pray that you will not
fall into temptation. The spirit is willing, but the flesh
is weak."

42 Once more Jesus went away and prayed, "My Father, if this cup of suffering cannot be taken away unless I drink it, your will be done." 43He returned once more and found the disciples asleep; they could not keep their eyes open.

44 Again Jesus left them, went away, and prayed the third time, saying the same words. 45Then he returned to the disciples and said, "Are you still sleeping and resting? Look! The hour has come for the Son of Man to be handed over to the power of sinful men. 46Get up, let us go. Look, here is the man who is betraying me!"

The Arrest of Jesus
(Mark 14.43-50; Luke 22.47-53; John 18.3-12)

47 Jesus was still speaking when Judas, one of the twelve disciples, arrived. With him was a large crowd armed with swords and clubs and sent by the chief priests and the elders. 48The traitor had given the crowd a signal: "The man I kiss is the one you want. Arrest him!"

49 Judas went straight to Jesus and said, "Peace be with you, Teacher," and kissed him.

50 Jesus answered, "Be quick about it, friend!"z

Then they came up, arrested Jesus, and held him tight. 51One of those who were with Jesus drew his sword and struck at the High Priest's slave, cutting off his ear. 52"Put your sword back in its place," Jesus said to him. "All who take the sword will die by the sword. 53Don't you know that I could call on my Father for help, and at once he would send me more than twelve armies of angels? 54But in that case, how could the Scriptures come true which say that this is what must happen?"

55 Then Jesus spoke to the crowd, "Did you have to come with swords and clubs to capture me, as though I were an outlaw? Every day I sat down and taught in the Temple, and you did not arrest me. 56But all this has happened in order to make what the prophets wrote in the Scriptures come true."

Then all the disciples left him and ran away.

zBe quick about it, friend! or Why are you here, friend?

Jesus Before the Council
(Mark 14.53–65; Luke 22.54–55, 63–71; John 18.13–14, 19–24)

57 Those who had arrested Jesus took him to the
house of Caiaphas, the High Priest, where the teachers
of the Law and the elders had gathered together.
58 Peter followed from a distance, as far as the courtyard of the High Priest's house. He went into the
courtyard and sat down with the guards to see how
it would all come out. 59 The chief priests and the
whole Council tried to find some false evidence against
Jesus to put him to death; 60 but they could not find
any, even though many people came forward and told
lies about him. Finally two men stepped up 61 and
said, "This man said, 'I am able to tear down God's
Temple and three days later build it up again.' "

62 The High Priest stood up and said to Jesus, "Have
you no answer to give to this accusation against you?"
63 But Jesus kept quiet. Again the High Priest spoke
to him, "In the name of the living God I now put
you on oath: tell us if you are the Messiah, the
Son of God."

64 Jesus answered him, "So you say. But I tell
all of you: from this time on you will see the Son
of Man sitting on the right of the Almighty and coming
on the clouds of heaven!"

65 At this the High Priest tore his clothes and said,
"Blasphemy! We don't need any more witnesses! You
have just heard his blasphemy! 66 What do you think?"

They answered, "He is guilty and must die."

67 Then they spat in his face and beat him; and
those who slapped him 68 said, "Prophesy for us,
Messiah! Guess who hit you!"

Peter Denies Jesus
(Mark 14.66–72; Luke 22.56–62; John 18.15–18, 25–27)

69 Peter was sitting outside in the courtyard when
one of the High Priest's servant-girls came to him
and said, "You, too, were with Jesus of Galilee."

70 But he denied it in front of them all. "I don't
know what you are talking about," he answered; 71 and
went on out to the entrance of the courtyard. Another

servant-girl saw him and said to the men there, "He was with Jesus of Nazareth."

72 Again Peter denied it and answered, "I swear that I don't know that man!"

73 After a little while the men standing there came to Peter. "Of course you are one of them," they said. "After all, the way you speak gives you away!"

74 Then Peter said, "I swear that I am telling the truth! May God punish me if I am not! I do not know that man!"

Just then a cock crowed, 75 and Peter remembered what Jesus had told him: "Before the cock crows, you will say three times that you do not know me." He went out and wept bitterly.

Jesus Is Taken to Pilate
(Mark 15.1; Luke 23.1-2; John 18.28-32)

27 Early in the morning all the chief priests and the elders made their plans against Jesus to put him to death. 2 They put him in chains, led him off, and handed him over to Pilate, the Roman governor.

The Death of Judas
(Acts 1.18-19)

3 When Judas, the traitor, learnt that Jesus had been condemned, he repented and took back the thirty silver coins to the chief priests and the elders. 4 "I have sinned by betraying an innocent man to death!" he said.

"What do we care about that?" they answered. "That is your business!"

5 Judas threw the coins down in the Temple and left; then he went off and hanged himself.

6 The chief priests picked up the coins and said, "This is blood money, and it is against our Law to put it in the temple treasury." 7 After reaching an agreement about it, they used the money to buy Potter's Field, as a cemetery for foreigners. 8 That is why that field is called "Field of Blood" to this very day.

9 Then what the prophet Jeremiah had said came true: "They took the thirty silver coins, the amount the people of Israel had agreed to pay for him, 10 and

used the money to buy the potter's field, as the Lord had commanded me."

Pilate Questions Jesus
(Mark 15.2–5; Luke 23.3–5; John 18.33–38)

11 Jesus stood before the Roman governor, who questioned him. "Are you the king of the Jews?" he asked.

"So you say," answered Jesus. 12 But he said nothing in response to the accusations of the chief priests and elders.

13 So Pilate said to him, "Don't you hear all these things they accuse you of?"

14 But Jesus refused to answer a single word, with the result that the Governor was greatly surprised.

Jesus Is Sentenced to Death
(Mark 15.6–15; Luke 23.13–25; John 18.39—19.16)

15 At every Passover Festival the Roman governor was in the habit of setting free any one prisoner the crowd asked for. 16 At that time there was a well-known prisoner named Jesus Barabbas. 17 So when the crowd gathered, Pilate asked them, "Which one do you want me to set free for you? Jesus Barabbas or Jesus called the Messiah?" 18 He knew very well that the Jewish authorities had handed Jesus over to him because they were jealous.

19 While Pilate was sitting in the judgement hall, his wife sent him a message: "Have nothing to do with that innocent man, because in a dream last night I suffered much on account of him."

20 The chief priests and the elders persuaded the crowd to ask Pilate to set Barabbas free and have Jesus put to death. 21 But Pilate asked the crowd, "Which one of these two do you want me to set free for you?"

"Barabbas!" they answered.

22 "What, then, shall I do with Jesus called the Messiah?" Pilate asked them.

"Crucify him!" they all answered.

23 But Pilate asked, "What crime has he committed?"

Then they started shouting at the top of their voices: "Crucify him!"

24 When Pilate saw that it was no use to go on,

but that a riot might break out, he took some water,
washed his hands in front of the crowd, and said,
"I am not responsible for the death of this man!
This is your doing!"

25 The whole crowd answered, "Let the punishment
for his death fall on us and our children!"

26 Then Pilate set Barabbas free for them; and after
he had Jesus whipped, he handed him over to be
crucified.

The Soldiers Mock Jesus
(Mark 15.16–20; John 19.2–3)

27 Then Pilate's soldiers took Jesus into the governor's palace, and the whole company gathered round
him. 28They stripped off his clothes and put a scarlet
robe on him. 29Then they made a crown out of thorny
branches and placed it on his head, and put a stick
in his right hand; then they knelt before him and
mocked him. "Long live the King of the Jews!" they
said. 30They spat on him, and took the stick and
hit him over the head. 31When they had finished mock-
ing him, they took the robe off and put his own
clothes back on him. Then they led him out to crucify
him.

Jesus Is Crucified
(Mark 15.21–32; Luke 23.26–43; John 19.17–27)

32 As they were going out, they met a man from
Cyrene named Simon, and the soldiers forced him
to carry Jesus' cross. 33They came to a place called
Golgotha, which means, "The Place of the Skull."
34There they offered Jesus wine mixed with a bitter
substance; but after tasting it, he would not drink
it.

35 They crucified him and then divided his clothes
among them by throwing dice. 36After that they sat
there and watched him. 37Above his head they put
the written notice of the accusation against him: "This
is Jesus, the King of the Jews." 38Then they crucified
two bandits with Jesus, one on his right and the
other on his left.

39 People passing by shook their heads and hurled
insults at Jesus: 40"You were going to tear down

the Temple and build it up again in three days! Save
yourself if you are God's Son! Come on down from
the cross!"

41 In the same way the chief priests and the teachers
of the Law and the elders jeered at him: 42 "He saved
others, but he cannot save himself! Isn't he the king
of Israel? If he comes down off the cross now, we
will believe in him! 43 He trusts in God and claims
to be God's Son. Well, then, let us see if God wants
to save him now!"

44 Even the bandits who had been crucified with
him insulted him in the same way.

The Death of Jesus
(Mark 15.33–41; Luke 23.44–49; John 19.28–30)

45 At noon the whole country was covered with
darkness, which lasted for three hours. 46 At about
three o'clock Jesus cried out with a loud shout, *"Eli,
Eli, lema sabachthani?"* which means, "My God, my
God, why did you abandon me?"

47 Some of the people standing there heard him
and said, "He is calling for Elijah!" 48 One of them
ran up at once, took a sponge, soaked it in cheap
wine, put it on the end of a stick, and tried to make
him drink it.

49 But the others said, "Wait, let us see if Elijah
is coming to save him!"

50 Jesus again gave a loud cry and breathed his
last.

51 Then the curtain hanging in the Temple was torn
in two from top to bottom. The earth shook, the
rocks split apart, 52 the graves broke open, and many
of God's people who had died were raised to life.
53 They left the graves, and after Jesus rose from death,
they went into the Holy City, where many people
saw them.

54 When the army officer and the soldiers with
him who were watching Jesus saw the earthquake
and everything else that happened, they were terrified
and said, "He really was the Son of God!"

55 There were many women there, looking on from
a distance, who had followed Jesus from Galilee and
helped him. 56 Among them were Mary Magdalene,

Mary the mother of James and Joseph, and the wife
of Zebedee.

The Burial of Jesus
(Mark 15.42–47; Luke 23.50–56; John 19.38–42)

57 When it was evening, a rich man from Arimathea
arrived; his name was Joseph, and he also was a
disciple of Jesus. 58He went into the presence of Pilate
and asked for the body of Jesus. Pilate gave orders
for the body to be given to Joseph. 59So Joseph took
it, wrapped it in a new linen sheet, 60and placed
it in his own tomb, which he had just recently dug
out of solid rock. Then he rolled a large stone across
the entrance to the tomb and went away. 61Mary
Magdalene and the other Mary were sitting there,
facing the tomb.

The Guard at the Tomb

62 The next day, which was a Sabbath, the chief
priests and the Pharisees met with Pilate 63and said,
"Sir, we remember that while that liar was still alive
he said, 'I will be raised to life three days later.' 64Give
orders, then, for his tomb to be carefully guarded
until the third day, so that his disciples will not be
able to go and steal the body, and then tell the people
that he was raised from death. This last lie would
be even worse than the first one."

65 "Take a guard," Pilate told them; "go and make
the tomb as secure as you can."

66 So they left and made the tomb secure by putting
a seal on the stone and leaving the guard on watch.

The Resurrection
(Mark 16.1–10; Luke 24.1–12; John 20.1–10)

28 After the Sabbath, as Sunday morning was dawn-
ing, Mary Magdalene and the other Mary went
to look at the tomb. 2Suddenly there was a violent
earthquake; an angel of the Lord came down from
heaven, rolled the stone away, and sat on it. 3His
appearance was like lightning, and his clothes were
white as snow. 4The guards were so afraid that they
trembled and became like dead men.

5 The angel spoke to the women. "You must not

be afraid," he said. "I know you are looking for Jesus, who was crucified. [6]He is not here; he has been raised, just as he said. Come here and see the place where he was lying. [7]Go quickly, now, and tell his disciples, 'He has been raised from death, and now he is going to Galilee ahead of you; there you will see him!' Remember what I have told you."

8 So they left the tomb in a hurry, afraid and yet filled with joy, and ran to tell his disciples.

9 Suddenly Jesús met them and said, "Peace be with you." They came up to him, took hold of his feet, and worshipped him. [10]"Do not be afraid," Jesus said to them. "Go and tell my brothers to go to Galilee, and there they will see me."

The Report of the Guard

11 While the women went on their way, some of the soldiers guarding the tomb went back to the city and told the chief priests everything that had happened. [12]The chief priests met with the elders and made their plan; they gave a large sum of money to the soldiers [13]and said, "You are to say that his disciples came during the night and stole his body while you were asleep. [14]And if the Governor should hear of this, we will convince him that you are innocent, and that you will have nothing to worry about."

15 The guards took the money and did what they were told to do. And so that is the report spread round by the Jews to this very day.

Jesus Appears to His Disciples
(Mark 16.14–18; Luke 24.36–49; John 20.19–23; Acts 1.6–8)

16 The eleven disciples went to the hill in Galilee where Jesus had told them to go. [17]When they saw him, they worshipped him, even though some of them doubted. [18]Jesus drew near and said to them, "I have been given all authority in heaven and on earth. [19]Go, then, to all peoples everywhere and make them my disciples: baptize them in the name of the Father, the Son, and the Holy Spirit, [20]and teach them to obey everything I have commanded you. And I will be with you always, to the end of the age."

THERE'S MORE GOOD NEWS TO READ

After

**Good News
told by Matthew**

Read

**Good News
New Testament**

75p **Post Free***

With index, word list and 100 illustrations

- -

To: The Bible Society
146 Queen Victoria Street, London EC4V 4BX
or
7 Hampton Terrace, Edinburgh EH12 5XU

Please send me **POST FREE** a **GOOD NEWS NEW TESTAMENT**. I enclose a cheque/P.O. for 75p

NAME: MR/MRS/MISS_____

ADDRESS:_____

_____

POSTCODE:_____

*While stocks last